T0318253

Politics and Economics in the History of the European Union

Britain's continued presence in the European Union has provoked debate, not only amongst the general public but also amongst academics. There is continued confusion amongst academics as to the nature and purpose of the European Union; does the EU exist for economic or political reasons?

This book uses an interdisciplinary approach to examine the nature and the scope of political and economic choice within the EU in order to provide the reader with a greater understanding of the motivation of new and existing member states. Alan Milward shows that the popular or academic judgement of the advantages and disadvantages of membership must be based on a political-economic judgement.

Politics and Economics in the History of the European Union will prove essential reading for students studying economics, international trade and European politics.

Alan S. Milward, Professor Emeritus of the London School of Economics, has taught history and economics in six countries and is external Professor of the European University Institute.

The Graz Schumpeter Lectures

For more information please visit the Graz Schumpeter Society's website:
www.uni-graz.at/vwlwww/schumpeter/schumpeter.html

Politics and Economics in the History of the European Union

Alan S. Milward

Routledge
Taylor & Francis Group

LONDON AND NEW YORK

First published 2005 by Routledge
2 Park Square, Milton Park, Abingdon, Oxon OX14 4RN

Simultaneously published in the USA and Canada
by Routledge
711 Third Avenue, New York, NY 10017

Routledge is an imprint of the Taylor & Francis Group, an informa business

First issued in paperback 2012

© 2005 Graz Schumpeter Society

Typeset in Times by
HWA Text and Data Management, Tunbridge Wells

British Library Cataloguing in Publication Data
A catalogue record for this book is available from the
British Library

Library of Congress Cataloging in Publication Data
A catalog record for this book has been requested

ISBN 13: 978-0-415-65389-3 (pbk)
ISBN 13: 978-0-415-32941-5 (hbk)

Contents

Illustrations

Figures

Tables

Preface

This book is based on the Joseph Schumpeter Lectures which I gave at the University of Graz. In academic life Schumpeter would now probably be classed as a 'political economist', but that was not the sole reason why these lectures were conceived as an argument that only an effort to write a political economy of the European Union will explain its history, its purposes, the way it has grown, and the way it functions. There was another reason. I had become weary of reading that my earlier works on its history presented the view that the European Union's origins were economic, whereas they have merely invited historians to write a broader history of the European Community/European Union than the diplomatic history, most frequently national diplomatic history, which remains their preferred choice. The lectures were an experiment in trying to explain the expansion of the European Community/European Union by as many avenues as I felt myself able, imperfectly, to explore. It was written in the hope of encouraging other historians to take the same risks, but also of encouraging social scientists and even, perhaps, journalists to meditate on the complexity, not reducible to simplifications, of a political development which has enfolded the lives of Europeans for half a century.

Each of the three chapters of this book is an exploration of the nature of national choice about and within the common market. As the purposes of the common market have been inseparably both political and economic, so has the nature of national policy choice about entering it and deciding policy objectives within it. This will remain so while national and supranational government both endure. There is very little to suggest that they will not both endure. In the search for an understanding of the politico-economic base of decision-making within the European Union, history, politics and economics have a common theoretical concern and a common descriptive purpose, to construct a political economy of policy choice. This could be a better guide to the compatibility of two-tier government with national democracy than theories and prognostications derived from one discipline only.

I wish to thank Stephan Boehm for his forbearance when bad health meant that I produced this book more slowly than I had intended. I would also like, in thanking the Economics Department of the University of Graz for their generous hospitality, to say that I was never elsewhere questioned so keenly with such courtesy. In many aspects it is difficult to imagine a more appropriate city from which to contemplate Europe's political economy.

Abbreviations

AASM	Associated African States and Madagascar
ACP	African, Caribbean and Pacific (signatories of the Lomé Conventions)
AEAM	Association des Etats Africains et Malgache
CAP	Common Agricultural Policy (of the EEC/EC/EU)
CET	Common External Tariff (of the EEC/EC/EU)
CFP	Common Foreign Policy (of the EEC/EC/EU)
CSCE	Conference on Security and Cooperation in Europe
DG	Directorate-General (of the European Community)
EC	European Community
ECJ	European Court of Justice
ECSC	European Coal and Steel Community
EDF	European Development Fund
EEC	European Economic Community
EFTA	European Free Trade Association
EU	European Union
FCO	Foreign and Commonwealth Office
GATT	General Agreement on Trade and Tariffs
IMF	International Monetary Fund
ITO	International Trade Organisation
Mercosur	Mercado Común del Sur
MFN	most favoured nation (clause in tariff agreements)
NA	National Archives (of the United Kingdom)
NAFTA	North American Free Trade Area
OECD	Organisation for European Cooperation and Development
OEEC	Organisation for European Economic Cooperation
SITC	Standard International Trade Classification
UK	United Kingdom of Great Britain and Northern Ireland
UNCTAD	United Nations Conference on Trade and Development
USA	United States of America

1 Economics and politics in the decision to join the European Union

The most successful aspect of post-war Europe's integration, the one that gives it genuine power and leverage in the world, which by its commercial power and attraction binds to the European Union (EU) most of the European states which are not members of it, is the common market. Excluding the value of the cross-border trade within the common market from the calculation, that is to say by assuming the EU to be one nation for trading purposes, it accounted in 2001 for 19.5 per cent of the total value of the world's exports and for 19.0 per cent of the world's imports. Were it one nation, it would be the world's greatest exporter. On the same basis the USA accounted in the same year for 15.7 per cent of world exports and 23.7 per cent of world imports.[1]

Even in citing that figure we are at once brought face to face with the fact that, no matter how mighty the economic weight of the European Union in commercial negotiations, it is not one nation. Although within the common market there are no tariffs, there remain other barriers and controls of various kinds on cross-border trade. Agricultural trade within and beyond the EU remains, in particular, tightly governed by the regulations of the Common Agricultural Policy (CAP) of the EU and within the Union is subject to frontier 'levies', whose purpose is to equalise foodstuff prices and to provide revenue for the administration of the Community. The difference between them and tariffs is more one of constitutional implication than of economic effect. Because its founding charter, the Treaty of Rome (1956), decrees that it is the European Commission, the European Community's executive, which shall conduct trade negotiations with other states, the Union comes much closer to acting like a single nation, at least in appearances, in international trade than in any other aspect of its activities. The reality, however, is that its component states closely supervise any action on the part of the Union's own trade negotiators. While it is statistically logical not to count as EU exports national exports to another country within the Union's boundaries, when they are reckoned as exports France, Germany, Italy and the United Kingdom are each numbered among the world's six biggest traders. That fact alone gives some measure of the magnitude of the common market's commercial leverage. It also makes the point that so huge a value and volume of cross-border trade within the common market cannot sensibly be separated from the structure and pattern of its trade with the external world. If we include trade between member-states of the EU in the calculation, counting it as a part of foreign trade, the EU was responsible in 2001 for 24.03 per cent of the value of all world exports.

In the purely political sphere, by contrast, the European Union has only a fleeting and rarely united world presence. It repeatedly fails to achieve agreement on common foreign policy objectives. When it does agree, the agreement is usually limited to platitudinous statements with which it is difficult to disagree but which are frequently equally difficult to act on. It cannot by itself defend its member-states if they are attacked by a greater power, for it effectively has only independent national armed forces to call on, most of them inadequate for the common task, should they, indeed, deem it a common task. Those states which joined in 2004 might often disagree with such elements of a common foreign policy as the EU of 2003 could occasionally tack together. Outside the commercial realm other aspects of economic policy remain often divisive. This is even the case for monetary and fiscal policy in spite of the monetary union. Neither France nor Germany intend in 2004 to abide by the rules for monetary policy which they themselves laid down and it may well be that they are wiser to honour in the breach the agreement on which they insisted rather than in the understanding.

It is true that the EU has succeeded in laying down political principles for new member-states, principally to ensure that democratic government endures, although some older member-states do not seem to apply these quite so strictly to themselves. The citizens of the European Union of fifteen states as it stood in 2003 see nevertheless its political machinery as distant from them, hard to comprehend, and insufficiently democratic. The European Parliament is elected by so small a percentage of the voters, and one which has diminished in every European election since the first, that it is hard to make a convincing case that its powers *vis-à-vis* the executive should be increased. The national populations, when questioned, vary between expressing only a weak allegiance to the Union or showing a substantial measure of distaste for it.[2] To be against dictatorship is a long way from perfecting democracy. Accepting that the majestic and mostly virtuous optimism of the political project to unite Europe in a common democracy has its own appeal, it is nevertheless tempting to conclude at first glance that the answer to the question posed by this chapter is that it must be the common market which causes states to seek membership of the European Union, because all other aspects of the Union are so frail.

There is a substantial body of economic theory which lends support to that answer and even goes beyond it in implying that the economic pressures imposed by a customs union on neighbouring countries will eventually lead to the expansion of the union by their absorption. At the time when post-Second World War opinion in the United States government was swinging, as a result of the Cold War and of the Marshall Plan, in favour of a customs union in western Europe and even contemplating this as a step towards some form of European political union in the distant future, Jacob Viner published a work which initiated theoretical analysis of the effects of customs unions and which remains an important point of reference.[3]

Viner divided the effects of the formation of a customs union into what he called 'trade creation' and 'trade diversion'. Trade creation he defined as the net addition to the previously existing value of a country's foreign trade ascribable to the reduction of barriers to trade as a result of its entry into a customs union. Trade diversion he defined as an increase of trade with other members of the customs union at the expense of a reduction of trade between the customs union and countries outside its boundaries. An increase in the absolute value of trade caused by trade creation would generate a net gain in welfare, derived, for example, from the substitution of lower cost material inputs into production or of other final cost reductions due to the removal of tariffs. Trade diversion implied the opposite effect. The preferment of inputs from within the customs union, whether for reasons of contiguity, implicit preferences, closer business connections, or the fact that some national tariffs might have to be adjusted upwards to achieve a common tariff, might mean in some cases that an increase in intra-trade within the union reached at the expense of non-union trade partners would lead to a reduction in total welfare.

With the notable exception of Greece in 1981 the expansion of the European common market has been through its absorption of closely neigh-bouring, in many cases contiguous, countries. The outcome has been that the imports of its member-states from each other have risen from 35 per cent of their total value to 60 per cent on the eve of its expansion in 2004 to include the former Soviet bloc states (Tables 1.1 and 1.2).

Viner pointed out that free traders and protectionists alike thought that customs unions in general supported their cause. Gillingham in his recent partisan history of post-war European integration, proclaiming the European Economic Community (EEC) as a massive step on the road to a free trade world which has brought great benefits, is at the same time unsparing of the protectionism on which its strength depended before the 1980s.[4] Viner argued that a customs union did have certain inbuilt protectionist advantages. The value of the common market's internal trade is greater now than that of its external trade, even after what Gillingham regards as fifteen years of the spread of 'free trade' beyond its frontier. EU states' imports from inside the

Table 1.1 Expansion of the EC/EU

1973	Entry of Denmark, Ireland, United Kingdom
1981	Entry of Greece
1986	Entry of Portugal, Spain
1995	Entry of Austria, Finland, Sweden
2004	Entry of Republic of Cyprus, Czech Republic, Estonia, Hungary, Latvia, Lithuania, Malta, Poland, Slovak Republic, Slovenia

Table 1.2 Intra-common market imports as a proportion of total imports (%)

1958	35.23
1972	53.83
1973	53.43
1980	49.23
1981	48.48
1985	53.36
1986	59.78
1994	60.76
1995	62.11
2001	59.45

Source: *Eurostat*, External Trade and Balace of Payments. *Statistical Yearbooks.*

Union have grown as a percentage of total EU imports internal and external, so that they now constitute well over a half. There is one clear cause of this trend: the physical area of the common market has expanded. Although the share of intra-trade imports in total imports occasionally shrank due to recession, as in the first year of the United Kingdom's membership, the overall trend has been that the greater the physical territory of the common market, the greater its level of self-sufficiency. It should be noted, however, that in the 1970s and early 1980s imports from outside the common market competed successfully with equivalent goods traded inside the market. It was mainly to Japan and the USA that the EC was losing ground in its own market, a situation reversed in the late 1980s and afterwards.

Because of restraints on labour mobility imposed by national welfare systems, by national subsidisation of agriculture (one of the policy purposes of which was to slow down the movement of labour out of agriculture), by linguistic and cultural differences between the national labour forces, and because, also, for much of the time of the lack of any unified capital market, the protectionist possibilities of a customs union, so Viner argued, as well as the possibilities of economic growth derived from scale economies, would in reality be more limited than theory predicted. Unaltered before the late

1980s, these realities did indeed mean that any comparisons between the USA and the EC revealed the common market not to have the advantages of a single, unified national market.[5] As it has acquired rather more of those advantages, so has its capacity to compete on its own territory with American and Japanese goods improved.

Most of the hypotheses which Viner used to build customs union theory depended on the tariff arrangements of any particular customs union, something which he readily acknowledged. For him the devil was in the detail. The lower the average level of the common tariff of the customs union compared to the averaged level of the national tariffs of its component states before the creation of the customs union, the nearer, he hypothesised, the customs union would be to obtaining the potential gains to welfare which could theoretically be expected from its formation. The detail, however, can be hard to determine. Whether the Common External Tariff (CET) of the common market was at first lower or higher than the average of the previous national tariffs of its constituent states was a matter of dispute. The United Kingdom appealed against its acceptance by the General Agreement on Trade and Tariffs (GATT) on the grounds that GATT rules forbade the formation of any customs union whose tariff was an increase on the average of the previously existing tariffs. The United States, for political reasons, rammed the change through GATT irrespective of the evidence that it may indeed have been a breach of the rules.

It was also the case, Viner hypothesised, that the greater the degree of competition between producers of high-cost products in the constituent states, the more was a customs union likely to generate some of the welfare gains of free trade. There was, however, he argued, also a countervailing tendency to this possibility; a customs union could move more quickly towards free trade with the external world the wider were the variations in unit costs of production in similar protected industries within its constituent states, because of the greater economies to be derived from internal trade within the union. By extension this implied that the gains to welfare would be greater the higher the tariffs protecting markets outside the union. By further extension, the greater the gains through increased sales of those same industries, the greater also the gain through a reduction in imports of the same products from outside the union.

These were hypotheses of possible outcomes from the formation of a customs union, strengthening the argument which Viner advanced more generally that a customs union had ample scope to seek gains to welfare both through protection and through free trade. In this argument 'protection' and 'free trade' were the two extreme points of a line, too extreme to be attainable by an institution which must by its nature be a complicated political compromise. Like Platonic ideals they could, however, serve as guides to action on earth. For a large economy, such as the United Kingdom, disposed by its previous experience to move towards 'free trade' as the better source of welfare gains, joining a customs union might well be a sub-optimal choice. Such it was, indeed, considered by the United Kingdom in the 1950s, as it was at the same time by the German Federal Republic's Minister of the Economy, Ludwig Erhard. In both cases the judgement was primarily economic although for both countries primary economic considerations led to political considerations which could be decisive in the other direction, as they were in the German case and as they became in 1961 in the British case.

From May 1960 the common market had a rival which proclaimed itself nearer to the 'free trade' point by its name, the European Free Trade Association (EFTA). Of EFTA, a British-inspired creation, Erhard took a favourable view, because he thought the gains which would accrue to Germany from a common market, within which France would have a long list of gains to be realised through cleaving closer to the protectionist point, would be less in total value than those from a joint venture with Britain towards the free trade point. He was prone to overestimating the propensities of Scandinavian countries to lean in the free trade direction and the ability of the United Kingdom to sustain the same course. In any case, because EFTA was created to pursue tariff and trade control bargaining with the common market, the difference in the nature of the two institutions had little significance for their respective tariff levels. EFTA's task was to track the common market's tariff projectory, a challenge which did not embarrass the EEC. The common market remained distinguished by its common economic policies, the Common Agricultural Policy, the Common Commercial Policy and Competition Policy, whose purposes were to equilibrate trading conditions within the market and to protect where necessary, but its external tariffs were on balance lower than those of many EFTA members on non-EFTA goods. It seemed to confirm Viner's view that it was able to realise the advantages both of trade liberalisation and of protectionism.

For small economies Viner implied that the most valid reason for joining either the common market or EFTA would be an economic one, access to a larger market within which they would reap the rewards from specialisation in niche products without fearing too severe an initial competition from outsiders. The situation for a smaller economy was, he implied, one in which it was probable that it would make more gains to welfare through membership than a larger economy. Experience in EFTA seems to bear this out. Five member-states saw the value of their exports within EFTA grow by far more than the average of all member-states over the years 1959–67 and for two others the figure was only a little below the average. The remaining member-state, the only large economy in EFTA, the United Kingdom, saw its exports grow over the same period by 92.0 per cent when the average for the whole association was 131.3 per cent.[6] Over the period 1959–63 British exports declined from 31.8 per cent of intra-EFTA exports to 26.4 per cent. All other countries increased their share.[7]

Considering therefore the answer to our question as it emerged from Viner's treatment of it, theory and practice seemed to offer one explanation for smaller economies to seek membership in some form of tariff union. The allocation of new trade to the headings of trade creation and trade diversion is, though, an imprecise procedure and the measurement of gains to trade is not without weaknesses in the historical perspective. Various methods of measuring 'new' trade have been tried. The two most frequently used techniques may be called the 'fixed shares' method and the 'extra-polation' method. The 'fixed shares' method would be to compare trade shares within the common market at given dates, before and after accession, with trade shares on other markets. A rise in intra-common market trade would be attributed to tariff preferences in any case where it was not matched by an increase in the share of imports from the common market by the outside market. The concept of the outside market as uninfluenced by, even independent from, the common market is, however, historically dubious. In the first twenty years of the common market, at the least, the growing share of exports by other member-states to Germany was partly dependent for its dimensions on Germany's exports to non-member-states. The extrapolation method extrapolates from a matrix of trade in a given year to compare the result with the actual trade flows in a later year. It is more difficult by this procedure to say what proportion of the difference between the real figures and the extrapolation is due to trade diversion, but as a method it has the advantage of using actual historical data as a comparator and it avoids the dubious idea of an inside world, the common market, and an outside world whose behaviour patterns are not influenced by each other.

The EFTA secretariat ventured into statistical efforts to separate trade creation, new trade, from trade diversion. Its efforts suggest that the poorest of its member-states, Portugal, did benefit from trade creation. It was, however, on particularly privileged terms in EFTA. About half of its imports from EFTA fell under an agreement, Annex G of the Stockholm Convention which created EFTA. For all the products in Annex G Portugal was allowed to reduce tariffs more slowly than the other member-states and even to create new tariffs to protect infant industries. Full tariff reduction within the rule for other EFTA members applied to only about one-third of Portuguese imports from them. Of the commodity groups which the secretariat was able to study, the growth of Portuguese exports within EFTA was only markedly characterised by trade creation in the case of textiles. This was probably not unconnected with the spread in the 1950s of non-tariff barriers to textile imports into European countries and the USA, from which Portuguese textile exports within EFTA, mostly to Britain, were exempt. This in itself is some evidence of the difficulties of turning Viner's theory into statistical fact. Trade creation effects were more evident for the highest per capita income EFTA member-state, Switzerland, than for the lowest, Portugal.[8] Nevertheless, no country's exports within EFTA grew so greatly as Portugal's and between 1957 and 1973, the year when the United Kingdom abandoned EFTA for the common market, the Portuguese economy experienced its highest rates of growth of GNP and of industrial product in the twentieth century.[9]

In the course of the two decades after he had written Viner's views were subjected to various theoretical criticisms which surely sprang from observation of the effects of the twenty years of exceptionally high economic growth rates of the member-states of both the common market and EFTA and from their apparent correlation with and causation by the equally exceptional growth rates of foreign trade. Notable in this criticism, for example, was the argument, made by Meade, that customs unions could generate gains to welfare not only by the generation of new trade but through their impact on patterns of consumption and prices.[10] Both he and Lipsey regarded Viner's assumption that real prices would remain constant as historically unrealistic, as indeed it was, and, therefore, the conclusion that changes in prices on the domestic markets reflected the impact of changes in tariffs as historically wrong. This made any precise calculation of gains to welfare from a customs union a much more difficult business and implied that they were contingent on a process of historical change of greater economic scope than the creation of a customs union. It might, Lipsey also noted, be the case that trade diversion, even if it did imply a shift to a more costly source of supply, might still lead to more trade in which the welfare gain from any given unit of trade might be smaller, but the total gain from all trade nevertheless be greater than before the formation of a customs union.[11] In short, Viner was simplifying history in the pursuit of theory.

Meade and Lipsey were introducing the historical reality of changes which they were currently observing into Viner's static assumptions. It was not only customs unions and free trade areas which altered the structure and pattern of western Europe's trade in the 1960s, the first decade of the customs union, it was the set of economic circumstances which had made it possible to have sustained growth of output at such high levels in western Europe in the 1950s, for it was that background which offered statesmen the possibility, not so common in human life, of choosing something desirable but safe. Tariff reduction and removal was the child of trade growth and economic growth, at least as much as it was their progenitor. This was one reason why studies of trade creation and trade diversion over periods of four to five years did not make any clear statement about the propensity of customs unions to generate higher rates of GNP growth through increased trade. The experience of almost the whole of western Europe after 1945 was of high rates of growth and GNP, even for countries outside the tariff unions and even for those with powerful trade controls such as Spain.

Viner's views, therefore, that for larger economies entry into a customs union might well be a sub-optimal economic choice and that such an economy was as likely, perhaps more likely, to seek to benefit from the protectionist possibilities of a customs union, were only partly appropriate to the quarter century of the great European boom. In the two most rapidly growing sectors of trade in manufactures, SITC (Standard International Trade Classification) 5 (chemicals) and SITC 7 (machinery and transport equipment) the sustained demand for German exports across the whole of western Europe led to a sustained demand from Germany for semi-manufactured imports, largely components of German exports, which in turn was a driving force in the industrialisation of less industrialised west European economies. This development of high-value, competitive intra-trade within the common market was matched by a parallel development within EFTA, with the German Federal Republic in both cases as the pivot of this growth of manufacturing output and trade. It was the fastest growing market for manufactured exports in SITC groups 5 and 7 for all mainland western European economies and their most rapidly growing supplier.[12] Intra-trade within the common market grew in value more for the most industrialised exporters, Germany, France and Belgium–Luxembourg. By contrast, it was agricultural trade, conducted within the regime of the Common Agricultural Policy (CAP) with its implicit commitment to Community preferences, which led to trade diversion. Over the period 1964–8 trade diversion for German agricultural trade was double the effect of trade creation.[13]

Given the impact of the common market on German, French and Italian trade within as well as outside the CET, compared to the United Kingdom's much less dynamic expansion of exports within EFTA, customs union theory looked an unsatisfactory predictor of what the attitudes of larger economies to joining a customs union should be. Becoming the flagship of a flotilla of smaller economies, as was Britain inside EFTA, confirmed Viner's early hypotheses; becoming the hub of a network of trade in manufactures in the geographical area where trade was growing most rapidly, the common market, as Germany did, radically altered them. This difference was one of the strongest influences on the British government in its decision to seek membership in the EEC, although it was certainly not the only one.

This change, however, has to be seen against the background of changing views of the ultimate purposes of the common market. In 1958, with the opening of the common market, Scitovsky published a short book comparing the benefits of a customs union with those of a complete economic union of western Europe with perfect mobility of labour and capital. The additional gains to welfare from the more complete economic union would, he concluded, be not much greater than those of the common market and would derive mostly from the same process, increased trade competition. Since that was so, there seemed little point in incurring the high costs of climbing the political mountain of a true economic union. Almost the same gains to welfare could be achieved by trade liberalisation alone. If the common market was but a step on the road to the 'free trade' end of Viner's line, the British government could envisage a destination shared with it. The political aspirations of the European Community would lose their force and purpose, or at least their more objectionable and threatening features would become merely postural rather than realisable. Huge political rearrangements did not warrant, so Scitovsky could be interpreted as saying, what could be achieved in the economic sphere by the continued process of trade liberalisation alone.[14]

Scitovsky's book might be seen from the present perspective as prescient. Had the political activity which created the first 'supranational' institutions of modern Europe and the shimmering, distant image of a politically united Europe which they preferred been no more than an extra motive force for reversing a process of trade restriction in western Europe which had reached its zenith in 1950? They are now susceptible of being interpreted as no more than a part of a greater change emanating from the commitment of American and European politicians in the 1950s to restore international economic relations to the pattern that prevailed from the mid-nineteenth century to the outbreak of the First World War.[15] Were that interpretation to be upheld, in spite of the massive simplification which it represents, the protectionist possibilities which Viner identified as inherent in customs unions and the web of theory which developed from his work would be of no more applicability than medieval angels counting their number on a pin head.

This would not mean that customs union theory loses all relevance to answering our question. Far from it, it remains one vital explanation of why countries do join customs unions. But it does mean that we must be clear about the nature of the institutional project which began with the Coal and Steel Community in 1950 and those others which have over half a century proliferated into 'regional' tariff unions and associations of various kinds; the Latin American Free Trade Area (LAFTA), Mercado Común del Sur (Mercosur), the North American Free Trade Agreement (NAFTA) and so on.

Why have such 'regional' associations flourished, particularly since the mid-1980s, when GATT already existed as a worldwide tariff negotiating institution before the birth of ECSC? Furthermore, over the time it took for the first 'Uruguay Round' of GATT negotiations to reach agreement, 1985–94, the European Union signed the European Economic Area (EEA) agreement with the remains of EFTA, accomplished two enlargements of its own geographical area, pursued a vigorous internal trade liberalisation of its own, agreed the terms of a monetary union and signed bilateral trade treaties with a number of other countries. The ensuing Uruguay Round of GATT ended in failure. That 'regional' trade institutions have become the most effective instruments of freeing trade, replacing the worldwide institutions for which the USA pressed in the reconstruction after the Second World War and that ECSC and the common market were the basis of this development, is inherent to Baldwin's argument that the common market is the prime cause of its own expansion.[16]

The essence of his argument is that 'deepening' of the EU, by which is meant the intensification of its internal integration, has provoked further widening of its frontiers. Thus the movement towards greater economic liberalisation within the common market in the 1980s culminating in the Single European Act saw that Act in its turn followed by the collapse of the Soviet bloc in eastern Europe and irresistible pressures on former eastern bloc and newly independent states to seek EU membership. This, he argues, was not a singular event in the expansion of the EEC/EU. Rather, so he claims, it was a typical and predictable one; 'idiosyncratic' shocks emanating from the EU common market have consistently generated demands for wider membership.

'Deepening' (*approfondissement*) has certainly been closely linked to the common market's expansion, but not necessarily in the sequence that Baldwin implies. The first expansion was determined by a prior agreement between the first six member-states to establish and fix for the long term the principles of a system of providing the Community with its own financial resources. These resources were to come from the levies at internal national frontiers inside the EU on agricultural trade. Since the purpose of the levies was to reach a common level of prices of agricultural products within the EU, the Community's 'own resources' were to be derived from fixing that common level of prices. In the case of the most important applicant, the United Kingdom, this was much more likely to deter expansion. The purpose of 'deepening' was in fact to create a set of common rules, some not wanted by the main applicant, before that applicant had any say in the matter or gained the power to change them. The CAP was defined as a fundamental part of the *acquis communautaire* which the new entrants must accept if there were to be any entry negotiations with them. This had no deterrent effect on Denmark and Ireland, quite the contrary in fact, but no applicant, and especially Norway and the United Kingdom, welcomed the further declaration, before their negotiations began, that there would be a Common

Fisheries Policy (CFP) to supplement the CAP. Far from bringing pressure to bear on Norway to join, this was an important cause of Norway's refusal of the terms of membership. There was no idiosyncratic shock from the common market which led to the UK's application for membership. The applications by Denmark, Ireland and Norway were largely determined by the importance to them of the British market, that is to say, by a shock emanating from Britain.

The ten states which joined in 2004 similarly had to accept in its entirety another stage of deepening. They must join the monetary union. They must give economic and political independence of action to their central banks. They must privatise most publicly owned industries and many services including telecommunications. The list is long and includes several nostrums which may prove only briefly fashionable. It is, in fact, more a characteristic of the EC/EU that it has intensified its internal coherence because additional states have sought membership, rather than that the progression of the Union persuaded or forced them to apply. This does not, however, mean that in a longer term context the success of the common market did not become a reason to seek membership.

Exclusion from the growing intra-trade of the common market was seen as holding down income growth in comparison with that in common market member-states. For a country still hoping to exercise worldwide economic and political influence, such as the United Kingdom, exclusion made both objectives more difficult. For smaller states, membership might involve a fuller recognition of their economic and political ambitions, or even, as in the case of Ireland, be seen as a full international acceptance of the country's political independence. In short, motives for accession were not lacking and idiosyncratic shocks emanating from the common market do not seem high among them.

Baldwin, it should be noted, is conscious that some political process is needed to move a state in the direction of seeking membership. He finds it in economic pressure groups, which, seeing exclusion as the sacrifice of improved marketing possibilities, bring pressure on government to change direction in favour of membership. The argument is a commonplace of political discussion and opinion and has received attention from historians. Their research seems to show that, as formulated by Baldwin, it is too general-ised an argument. To be effective it needs to be reduced to finer detail of which pressure groups and even which persons were able to exercise influence on governments. National federations of businessmen are seen from historical records to be extremely careful to represent the interests of all their various branches, so that their advice to government concentrates on being verbally 'pro-business' rather than overtly taking sides about what a pro-business foreign policy means. Thus German business leaders were divided in their attitudes to the common market proposal. While in principle in favour of the general idea, their detailed response varied according to the level of competition they expected.[17] Thus business leaders divided in the same way over the choice between the common market alone and the British proposal to associate it with an outer free trade area. Two important sectors of German industry, paper and board manufacturers and non-ferrous metal producers, were strongly opposed to the free trade area proposal that was looked on with some favour by the Ministry for the Economy, because they would have been unable to meet the price competition from Scandinavian countries likely to be in the free trade area. Chancellor Adenauer, who for political reasons did not want the common market blended into a free trade area, took the opportunity offered by those objectors, who may have been preferring a minority view among representatives of German business, to support the French veto on this particular form of 'widening'.[18]

The argument that business associations serve as pressure groups to activate the state to respond to the growth of the common market by joining it is plausible, but not proven and only as one form of a variety of political pressures in the same direction. Too much is at stake in such decisions for the political machinery of decision-making to be so simplified. Joining the common market to improve a country's political and economic prospects meant having some firm idea about what national policy should continue to be once it was inside the European Community framework.

Chapter 2 examines the way in which entry into the common market was seen in Denmark and Ireland as a way of furthering the domestic policy objective of industrialisation. Accession to the European Communities was not simply a response to the decision of their largest market, the United Kingdom, to apply for membership, although the British decision determined the timing of their application. Both were pursuing the specific objective of industrialisation in the context that liberalisation of trade required a greater output of manufactured exports, for which common market membership would provide the opportunity. Both countries were not simply absorbed by the growing pressure of the common market. Each had decided before the United Kingdom announced its intention to seek membership that with Britain inside the European Community the opportunity for a policy which strengthened their domestic industrial base would be presented.

Gains to trade may in fact have accrued to every new entrant into the common market. One reason for an immediate increase in exports to the common market brought about by entry is that each accession, except that of Greece, was to a common market also enlarged at the same time by the accession of other new member-states, but a comparison of the trade experience of new entrants to the common market suggests that many more complicated stories than that are to be told.

As a simple picture of the increased share of United Kingdom exports sold within the nine-country European Community, as it became at the start of 1973, Figure 1.1 shows that it took six years of membership for that share to return to its level of 1965. Exclusion from the common market and the trade discrimination which that entailed was an important cause in the decline in the share of British exports directed to the common market throughout the 1960s. To what extent the recouping of that share between 1974 and 1979 was ascribable to gains to trade, rather than to trade diversion, seems a narrow question compared to a more striking effect. From the start of 1974, as Figure 1.1 implies, the common market's impact was to redirect British exports towards its original six members and away from the two countries which joined the EEC on the same day as the United Kingdom: Denmark and Ireland. This should not be taken as a matter of course on the grounds that Denmark and Ireland were such small markets compared to the six original EEC member-states. Danish and Irish imports from the United Kingdom in the 1960s were a larger share than that of the Six. British goods imported into Ireland over the period 1966–72 exceeded the value of Italian imports from Britain and almost matched the value of those by France. The stability of Denmark's and Ireland's share of UK exports before 1973 was disrupted by UK entry into the Community, even though Denmark and Ireland entered at the same time. Britain re-entered a world of greater manufacturing sophistication and the more complex pattern of interchange and intra-trade in manufactured products which the common market facilitated.

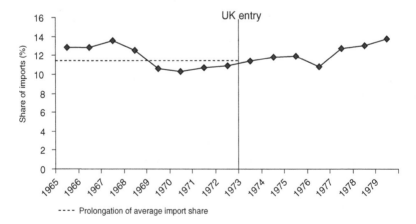

Figure 1.1   United Kingdom exports to the nine-country EC before and after accession as a share of total EC-nine intra-trade imports

Source: Eurostat, *External Trade, Statistical Yearbook* (1980: 50, 51).

If we look at the second expansion of the EEC, the entry of Greece, the overriding characteristic, before and after expansion, is the volatility of Greek exports. Mainly this volatility is to be ascribed to their small value, only 1.3 per cent of the total intra-trade imports of the Community in the year of Greece's accession, and to a lesser extent to their commodity composition, in which inessential foodstuffs and raw materials, of which other sources of supply existed, predominated.

Greece's situation was different from that of any other successful applicant for membership in that its Treaty of Association with the EEC had been specifically a treaty to prepare to sustain the economic transition to a more open economy which membership imposed. The complete restoration of the terms of the treaty in 1975 after the collapse of the military government did not make any difference, however, to the proportion of Greek exports sold within the common market. On the other hand, accession generated a steep increase in the proportion of total exports going to Community markets, but only for that increase to fall as steeply in the second three years of membership as it had risen in the first (Figure 1.2). In 1991 the share of Greek exports sold within the Community was lower than the average share over the years between the restoration in full of the Treaty of Association and Greek accession.

If we then compare Greece's experience to that of Spain and Portugal (Figures 1.3 and 1.4) we have a sufficiently different set of results to show

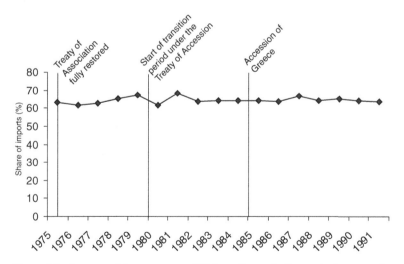

Figure 1.2   Imports of the ten-country EC from Greece before and after accession as a proportion of world imports from Greece

Source: Eurostat, *External Trade, Statistical Yearbook* (1992: 48, 50).

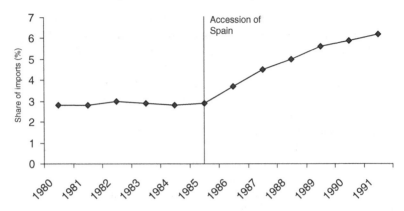

Figure 1.3   Twelve-country EC imports from Spain as a proportion of world imports from Spain before and after accession

Source: Eurostat, *External Trade, Statistical Yearbook* (1994: 10, 12).

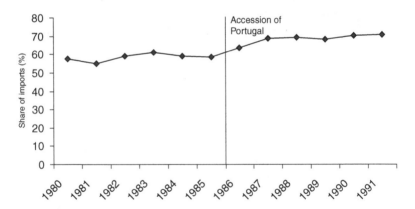

Figure 1.4   Twelve-country EC imports from Portugal as a proportion of world imports from Portugal before and after accession

Source: Eurostat, *External Trade, Statistical Yearbook* (1992: 48, 65).

how the historical experience of accession was in fact much more complicated, even if in general gains to trade were the outcome of accession, than customs union theory allows for.

No country entered abruptly into the EEC. The United Kingdom, Denmark and Portugal were members of EFTA before entering the common market, the first two for 12.5 years, Portugal for twenty-five years. Greece had had trade treaty relations with the common market for 19.5 years specifically shaped to bring it into the common market. Spain had preferential trading relations with the Community for sixteen years before accession. Ireland was not in EFTA and had no treaty relationship with the common market, but for six years before accession it had experienced the impact of a free trade treaty with the United Kingdom, intended to make entry into the common market economically less dislocating.

In the year before their accession Portugal and Spain had, respectively, more than a third and almost one half of their total exports already directed towards the common market. After accession the proportion of Spanish exports sold within the Community grew more steeply than before accession, while that of Portuguese exports did not. At the same time, however, there was a remarkable expansion of Portuguese–Spanish trade. For the five years before their accession Spain's imports from Portugal averaged 5.8 per cent of its annual imports from the twelve-country EEC; over the six years following accession the share climbed to 19.8 per cent, compared to an increase of only 3.9 per cent in the value of imports from the common market as a whole. This trend was to continue, so that underdeveloped Portugal was a major beneficiary of Spanish accession.

Portugal, like the United Kingdom, appears as a demonstration of the common market's capacity to diversify the geographical distribution of exports rather than to narrow it. Spain, whose formal relationship with the EC was much less intimate, had the highest proportion of its total exports going to the common market before accession of all the countries we are here comparing, yet on political grounds, strong for both Spain and the Community, its membership of the Community was unacceptable before 1986.

The economic experience of common market membership was, it would seem, heavily influenced by political circumstance. Ireland's political aloofness, the suspicions of the two authoritarian Iberian states of each other, the inherently difficult economic and political problems of the weakness of Greece's exports structure and the suspicions it aroused in the minds of Greek politicians that the Community might turn out to be yet another exploiter, the United Kingdom's anxieties that its world was narrowing through entry into the common market; all this array of political circumstance had historical origins, which, although they escape the grasp of customs union theory, influence the flow of trade.

Beyond these political considerations, the examples of Portugal and Ireland after accession show that access to a larger market was not necessarily the cause of the immediate increase in the value of exports to its members. It was also the capacity of a common market, or any customs union, to create a much greater and more complex mesh of intra-trade than was possible with variable national tariffs. The United Kingdom dominated the increase in Irish exports within the common market after its entry, as it had dominated

Irish exports before entry. Calculated by national destinations, the geographical distribution of Ireland's exports altered only slowly after its accession in 1972, but the pattern within which value was added in more than one country to exports originating from any member-state applied to Irish products as much as those of other member-states, making the United Kingdom a bridge to the continental market.

Propinquity, as trade theorists have belatedly recognised, is a weighty factor in the geographical distribution of trade. Portugal's high rate of export growth within EFTA had little to do with the very high growth rate of its neighbour Spain after 1958. Spain was not in EFTA and the Spanish market was strongly protected by import controls and other non-tariff barriers deriving from Franco's dictatorial government. Accession to the common market together for Portugal and Spain in 1986 meant Portugal's first fully liberalised access to the Spanish market. Over the first five years of the membership of both countries in the European Community the increase in the value of Portugal's exports to Spain was almost a quarter of the total value of its exports to the twelve-country Community. Spain was Portugal's bridge into the rest of the common market as the United Kingdom was Ireland's. The growth of Irish trade within the common market provides an even more striking example. In current values total trade grew at an average annual rate of 22.16 per cent over the first seven years of membership. To the nine-country EEC it grew at an annual average rate of 23.16 per cent. Exports to the United Kingdom in the same period were in every year around three-quarters of total exports to the EEC. In the three years before entry exports to Britain had made up more than 80 per cent of Ireland's total exports, so that accession to the EEC for Ireland made only a small impact on the recorded geographical distribution of its export trade, but the underlying lesson was that an increased share of British exports directed to the common market was bound to be helpful to Ireland. The share of United Kingdom exports in the imports of the countries which from 1 January 1973 constituted the nine-country common market dwindled persistently from 1963 to 1974. In 1975 it began to increase, and in 1979 already exceeded its share of 1965, climbing more steeply than it had fallen.

The longer term context was that the common market conducted after 1960 an increasing share of western Europe's foreign trade at a slightly, but persistently, higher average year-on-year percentage rate of improvement of real GDP per capita than that of European OECD member-states outside the market, and that with each territorial expansion of the common market its leverage in international trade bargaining grew. It is, nevertheless, a large leap in reasoning to conclude, as Baldwin does, that customs union theory has the explanatory power of a 'domino theory'.

Greece, for example, did not have the same experience as Spain, Portugal

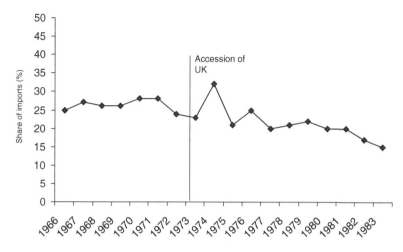

Figure 1.5 Danish and Irish imports from the UK as a proportion of the value of total nine-country EEC imports from the UK, 1966–83

Source: Eurostat, *External Trade, Statistical Yearbook* (1994).

and Ireland. Its exports were volatile, even though over 50 per cent of their value went to other member-states after Greek accession. The share of exports to the Community in total Greek exports did not behave like that of Spain or Portugal, as Figure 1.2 shows. Trading experience inside the European Community depended for small countries, as Chapter 2 suggests, on a purposive policy and that policy in turn on changing the commodity structure of exports. It is not evident that Greece had the wherewithal to change the commodity structure of its exports so purposefully. In such circumstances the increased efficiencies from entry into the larger market may not immediately present themselves. Setting aside political and historical considerations, there are variations in the possible economic responses to immersion in a larger, more liberalised market.

But there is a much more evident reason why European states were not merely dominoes waiting to fall down into line. It is that democratic states are political entities whose decision-making processes are majoritarian and for numerous weighty reasons the political issues assumed priority in their calculations. In any democracy, *whose* gain is the question which dominates the political argument. It is, certainly, theoretically possible in the case of countries seeking admission to the EC/EU to admit the possibility of a scenario where a large majority of the population of the applicant state stands to gain economically. There was one such case in the first expansion, that of Ireland. The scenario turned out to be exaggerated, but it proved nevertheless an acceptable approximation to the truth. Such an example does not alter the fact that, for all applicant countries in each successive expansion of the EC/EU, the fundamental economic questions for voters were questions of detail. The detailed questions about membership: who gains most, who gains least, who loses, are inescapably questions arising from and leading to political syntheses.

As the surrenders of sovereignty must be debated and different concepts of the nation paraded and argued over, it is within this debate that the search for a national political economy, which could mitigate the force of surrenders of national decision-making or preserve the nation from the less wanted repercussions of common sovereignty, emerges. The example of the United Kingdom is telling. The purpose of seeking accession was frequently said in public, as in secret government discussion, to be the improvement of the economy or even the arrest of economic decline. That argument was invariably accompanied by a seemingly separate argument that membership of the Community would enhance Britain's diminishing political influence in the world. The accompanying argument subsumed another argument that one purpose of improving economic performance was to wield greater political power. Only the narrowest of economic interest groups argued for membership solely on economic grounds. The counter-argument to the view that the United Kingdom would be surrendering both parliamentary sovereignty and national sovereignty by signing the Treaty of Rome was that to hold its place as the greatest of the non-superpowers those surrenders were necessary. An advantage gained from such a surrender was preferable to the loss of absolute independence, which in a world of superpowers was in any case a chimera. The advantage gained would be both political and economic. In its formulation the argument put before the British voters, and for that matter before the voters of other applicant countries, was therefore always a dynamic one; membership would permit, perhaps indeed compel, economic efficiencies unattainable in a smaller national market and from those efficiencies must spring higher rates of total factor productivity from which, in turn, would spring higher growth rates, and thus for voters higher real incomes and for the nation greater influence. The argument was irresistible for a nation which less than a century earlier had been the world's largest economy and where now the economic discussion was all about 'decline'.

It is in the way such arguments were framed to tap for support the electorate's subconscious anxieties that we can better understand why arguments for membership of the Community were always political syntheses in which economic calculations, no matter how importantly they weighed with certain groups, were never the predominant element that it might have seemed reasonable to expect they would be. Reasonable, certainly, in 1971, because of the four applicants, only one, Denmark, had shown any marked degree of positive interest in creating a politically united Europe. Most of that interest had been shown by members of one political party, Venstre, whose bedrock support came from larger farmers economically discriminated against by the fact that their biggest potential export market, Germany, was in a tariff union of which they were not a member.

The result of Denmark's campaign for membership was to leave relatively undisturbed the conclusion that, economically, membership would be good for Denmark, but also to awaken an increasingly persistent mood of political criticism of the loss of sovereignty involved in the choice. The Irish taoiseach (prime minister) Jack Lynch, who took his country into the Community, did not appeal to Ireland's long attachment to continental Europe as a potential intellectual and cultural liberator from British domination. He insisted in his speeches on the Community as a guarantee of major economic gains and talked about grain, beef and butter prices. He may have regretted the missed opportunity to awaken greater European emotions in the Irish soul. The less romantic message, however, produced a vote of 83 per cent in the required referendum in favour of the terms of accession. Even so, there was always the sub-text for Irish electors that entry into the European Community would eventually diminish their economic dependence on the United Kingdom and thus the extent of their continuing political subordination to it. Furthermore, it would do that harmlessly, because Britain would join at the same time. Ireland would thus incur no economic or political difficulties from any sudden break with the British market in what would be only a slowly widening separation.

There are evidently other reasons for the need for each application for entry into the EC/EU to be couched as a political argument. They are a mixture of the precise and the nebulous. The process of application, invented for the United Kingdom's first, failed application in 1961, has remained substantially unchanged. It was invented as a lengthy, detailed political process, begun by the applicant country making a statement of political approbation of and allegiance to the constitutional *acquis* of the European Communities, which is in fact still, at the moment of writing, not a constitution but only a working method. The conclusion of the negotiations is a deal, mostly over economic issues, but because each country does not enter under the same conditions the deal must be described as political, because the negotiations are lengthy and arouse strong political anxieties and hopes in the applicant countries.

Governments of applicant countries focus a massive presentational and public relations effort on the electorate to make sure that it will support entry. It is in this process, because the core of the argument resides in the question whether the surrender of sovereignty is worth the politico-economic gain which the government proclaims will accrue, that political issues come even more to the forefront. That cloudy concept, 'national identity', about which in the last decade so many books have been written without making its nature much clearer, becomes a touchstone of the decision to be made. In the acute circumstance that the decision for entry is perceived as a final one, not only because there is no mechanism in the Treaty of Rome for renouncing it but, more importantly, because the campaign for entry has to be a campaign for permanent membership if it is to be credible, the argument surpasses the form of a myriad of separate personal opinions. The two sides are forced into sketching out some rough model of what the future nation should be and do. When the accession campaigns are inspected in detail, arguments for and against membership frequently refer to political/economic conceptions of what the nation has been, now is, and could become.

While such mental constructs may be no more than romantic illusion or even fantasy, they are shaped in the case of accession by a precise issue raising precise questions which are indeed about the future of the nation. Consider in this context the first expansion of the EEC. In 1971 it seemed certain that incomes in the agricultural sector would gain from membership and strengthen the political weight of agriculture within the applicant state. It seemed that the evident desire of the European Commission to harmonise indirect taxation rates might have serious implications for the pattern of income distribution and welfare policies. The transition to conformity with the Common External Tariff and the accompanying removal of national tariffs within the Community necessarily involved shifts in the structure and geographical distribution of employment. So, too, it was feared, would the 'right of establishment' of businesses from other member-states. Regional policy, competition policy, social policy, all looked as though they too might become influential enough to alter the character and permissible range of government intervention in industry. Furthermore, all the new members had to sign up for the eventual monetary union whose stages were set out in the Werner Plan and thus for an eventual common monetary policy. Even though, as a result of the international monetary disorder which was the background to the early negotiations, the likelihood of monetary union receded, neither the idea nor the intention were abandoned.

Try though they did, the governments of the 1971 applicants could never convincingly argue to their electorates that all they were doing was joining what had become no more than another intergovernmental institutional organisation whose grandiose ideas of European Union had been firmly snuffed out by de Gaulle in the 1960s, so that all that was at stake was the acceptance of a common programme of trade liberalisation and greater freedom of movement for capital and people. Their efforts brought to life instead an enduring and critical discussion about whether the European Community was a belittlement of national democracy, an intolerable transfer of crucial powers of decision, won through many hard earlier battles, to a level of governance beyond the effective reach of national parliaments. Government responses, that the entry of four states which were beyond all questioning parliamentary democracies would in itself democratise the European Community structure, only emphasised the ambivalence of the arguments. Why would an international trading institution need a democratic parliament?

As the detail of the negotiations for entry, which within the convention of international diplomacy was kept as secret as possible, was nevertheless followed as intently as possible in each applicant state, aided by the leakiness of the Commission of the European Communities, the national debates were notable for the fundamental nature of their judgements. The first British application for membership of the Communities in 1961 was opposed by the leader of the Labour Party, Hugh Gaitskell, speaking at his party's annual conference as 'the end of a thousand years of history'. The reply from the Home Secretary, R.A. Butler, in the governing Conservative Party's annual conference in the same year was, 'For them a thousand years of history; for us the future.' This was a rare moment, when the full scope of the decision to be made was acknowledged by the government. Popular discussion of it, however, was much more frequently cast in such a categorical mode, even though before 1961 opinion on the question of accession had been too muted to have much impact on daily politics. No matter how carefully undramatic the government tried to keep the level of campaigning, the Gaitskell–Butler interchange was an acknowledgement that the public had got the point.

Consider the example of Norway, a model of governance by democratic ratiocination. Twice Norway reached an entirely democratic, national, central, parliamentary decision to apply for membership. Twice that decision was overwhelmed by adverse political currents swirling from an equally democratic local level, the depths of whose waters had not been adequately plumbed. That the referendum shipwreck of 1972 was repeated twenty-two years later is an eternal reminder that no democratic state's decisions can be solely a response to so automatically functioning and simple a calculus of economic gain and loss as customs union theory proposes, even when the combined efforts of pressure groups in a country with a population of only 4.4 million people are taken into account. If that is true for a country with so small a population whose foreign trade (exports plus imports) was more than a quarter of the value of its GDP and when that trade was mostly with the common market and its fellow applicants, it must be a potential scenario in larger states with a greater geographical diversity of exports.

In such circumstances the idea of a national political economy, the concept that there is some optimum economic balance which the state can reach by interventionist policies which would not weaken or endanger its democratic political system, a persistent idea in all recovery planning after 1945, was directly challenged by the very process of integration itself. Since, however, most west European states were for more than twenty years after 1945 achieving unprecedently high rates of growth under economic regimes which even in their most liberal examples retained extensive powers of economic direction, the idea that each state had an optimum national political economy which served as a rough political guide towards what economic intervention should aim at persisted. It persisted also in the European Community institutions themselves and was only seriously weakened at both national and supranational levels in the later 1970s when instability, unemployment and lower growth rates had re-established themselves.

Non-interventionist, free-trading models were always an alternative, but not until the later 1970s did they prevail and even then each national state within the European Community clung to its own persistent ideas of industrial management and the direction of investment. Because it was the business of competitive national political parties to present some composite image of national identity to the electorate, when the overall tendency of economic policy veered towards a more liberal 'globalisation', the images survived in opposition arguments and were taken out, honed, polished and purveyed during any campaign for accession to the European Community. They were, of course, arguments based on the need to exercise national government sovereignty. The year 1972 in the United Kingdom and Denmark provides good examples of linking the preservation of government powers over industrial, investment and social policy to rejecting Community membership. The campaign for a negative vote in the Norwegian referendum of that year is an even more telling example. Unsullied mountain landscapes, crystal-clear waterfalls, nationalist ballads and peasant folk singers in regional and national costume cluttered the Norwegian television screen. All seemed a long way from, and much healthier than, Brussels or Bonn. The European Commission, uncontrolled by an unelected parliament which met for short periods only, presented an easy target to opponents of membership in 1970–2 and an easy platform from which to focus their arguments on the need to preserve democracy within the nation.

After the 1973 expansion, international support for democracy became a publicly proclaimed objective of the Community. Spanish 'association' with the EEC by means of a trade treaty had raised opposition from some member-states as early as the 1950s on the grounds that a dictatorship should not be incorporated into a structure intended to strengthen the political unity and harmony of the West. The debate over the relationship between the European Communities and Spain, preceding any vigorous public discussions of the need to democratise the Communities, points to a more important origin of the European Union's eventual self-proclamation as a standard-bearer of international democracy than the pressure brought to bear on it by critics and opponents of expansion in the member-states. Its identification with democracy was embedded in its creation as a pillar of the European peace settlement of 1947–50, because in that settlement it was the substitute for the peace treaty that could not be signed.

The ECSC and the EEC were both created for a great political objective: to deal with the place and power of Germany in Europe. They were instruments to control Germany and to ensure the German Federal Republic's attachment to the western bloc countries. German reunion could come about only in a Europe where it no longer had threatening consequences for the western allies. To achieve that objective an armed western Europe had to stand steadfast against the Soviet threat. The political objective outweighed in importance, and was a precondition for, any schemes for political union. Because the immediate reasons for which the European Communities were founded outweighed in their urgency the submergence of the idea of the nation-state into a political union, that political union was thought of more as an eventual crowning symbol than as an urgent and necessary achievement. The search for economic gains from EU membership thus had to be based on two political necessities: not to weaken the foundation of the peace settlement, which meant accepting the long-run existence of the common market as a political institution; and standing ready to envisage some political 'deepening' of the common market. Few decisions about commercial policy could in this context be free from political implications of the most serious kind, distant though the implications might be.

A trade treaty with Spain was a politically conditioned proposal in the 1950s, because Spain was a military ally of the West and an absolute opponent of the communist regimes, but it was rejected because for some of the six EEC members, and notably Belgium, democracy was a necessary quality of a customs union which had to be envisaged as a possible future political union. Economic objections to the proposed treaty were inconsequent. The first 'Association Agreement' with a European non-member-state, was signed with Greece in 1961. It was specifically stated to have the purpose of preparing Greece for full Community membership. It was suspended, except for the continuing process of tariff reduction, after a military dictatorship took control in Athens on 21 April 1967 and was only restored to full operation on 17 September 1974 after the colonels were replaced by the Karamanlis government. The deaths of the two Iberian dictators, Salazar and Franco, were seen as the chance to bring dictatorship to an end in western Europe by stabilising and protecting parliamentary democracy in Portugal and Spain. The implication was that the same form of government must triumph in the eastern bloc if a truly European Union was to come into being.

The EC/EU moved from using the concept of democracy to reach negative decisions, proscribing dictatorships, to positive decisions, prescribing what constitutes a democracy, even if the population of Norway remained unconvinced that it was qualified to do so. The former eastern bloc countries who entered the EU in 2004 were faced with firm prescriptions for domestic political and economic change in order to gain accession. In one respect these prescriptions may be seen as no more than a repetition of earlier scenarios in which successful applicants had to accept the existing set of practices and policies of the West as represented by the Community. In their case these now included Economic and Monetary Union. If eastern bloc countries joined the Community, they would have to accept in full the *acquis communautaire*, which now had the status of a definition of democracy. Although much of what the *acquis* was composed of would not have appeared in any way in 1947 as integral to democratic government, it remained the case that what was at stake was the outlines of the European political settlement reached in 1950. Economic policy prescriptions could change, but the political settlement demanded that it change in the way the western states now saw as fundamental to democracy. National economic, fiscal and monetary policies now must provide the maximum liberty possible to the unfettered forces of the single market of the customs union. Because those policies remain disputed as a political foundation for democracy, alternative political economies of democracy will challenge the present definition and therefore also perhaps the European Union. But if these be mutable principles, their adoption only emphasises the more that the essential foundations of the common market remain political.

This point is reinforced by the links which the historical emphasis on democracy inside the customs union established with the emphasis on human rights and their recognition by the applicant states in the Conference on Security and Cooperation in Europe (CSCE) at its Helsinki meetings, although no clear historical path has yet been traced as to how human rights became so important in the agreements to which the Conference came. The Treaties of Paris and Rome established some economic rights for citizens of the signatory countries, the 'right of establishment' for instance. These were to be upheld by the European Court of Justice (ECJ). By 1970, however, the Court had established its own claim to protect some fundamental rights as an aspect of the Community's legal order. This position was only legitimised by Article 6 of the Treaty of Maastricht in 1992, after German reunification and after the Helsinki agreements on Peace and Security.[19] Nevertheless, the issue of human rights had become established within European Community law earlier than the Helsinki accord, because it had become evident that in practice the purely economic activities, which the Community treaties protected as a right, did in fact have an impact on human rights sufficient to provide some justification for the extension of its jurisdiction by the ECJ. The end of the Cold War was, nevertheless, the decisive moment.

Only when it was faced no longer with Soviet competition in the Third World did the European Union insert human rights conditions into its development aid contracts. Enlargement of the EU eastwards then obliged the existing member-states to define what they meant when they insisted that new member-states must be democratic. Their definitions became the so-called 'Copenhagen Criteria' for accession adopted by the Council of Ministers of the EU in summer 1993. The Treaty of Amsterdam amended the Rome Treaty on European Union (Article 6(1)) to declare that the EU was 'founded on the principles of liberty, democracy, respect for human rights and fundamental freedoms'.[20] Even though in some cases entrants are asked to conform to organisational and political norms to which existing member-states still do not fully conform, the essential point is that the conditions are seen as sustaining the European peace settlement in the new circumstances of a reunited and proportionately more powerful Germany.

When Soviet power and communist government collapsed in central and eastern Europe and in Russia from early 1989 onwards, all perspectives for the European Single Act and the European Union were enlarged but also threatened by the possibilities of German reunification and the greater freedom for Germany's foreign policy on its eastern frontiers. Prescriptions for freer markets within the EU had to come to terms with a set of crucial political decisions if the Union was still to be the coping-stone of Europe's peace settlement. It was in those circumstances that the EU's conditions for the accession of eastern bloc countries took on an international ideological hue rather than merely stating the economic rules as they by then existed. Freedom of commerce was linked to the economic policies which appeared to have won the Cold War and thence to democracy, as it had been by British statesmen in the mid-nineteenth century. The end of the Cold War has thus merely altered the vocabulary in which application for accession is made. The vocabulary and the new conditions remain heavily economic, their deepest intent remains political.

Lastly, to add a final emphasis to this point, it is well to remember that only when the future position of a reunited Germany had been placed under what controls the peace settlement could still muster were Europe's neutrals admitted into the European Union. Neutrality until then had been a position which presented in the minds of both neutrals and member-states serious obstacles to European Community membership and even to a commercial agreement which had any implication beyond that of a normal trade treaty. The Treaty of Association signed between Greece and the EC stipulated that the objective of association was eventual membership. Could the EC contemplate the same terms for a neutral country?

At first, for almost entirely economic reasons, the Swedish Conservative Party, the Liberal Party and the main businessmen's organisation supported, at the moment of Danish and Norwegian decisions to apply for membership, application for some form of association with the Community for Sweden. The Social Democrats were in danger of splitting over the issue. The Communists and the Centre Party opposed any eventual full membership. Anything less than full membership with the same political standing as other member-states was regarded by the Conservatives as not worth the surrender of sovereignty involved.[21] Other advocates of membership might have been satisfied with merely a trade agreement which would leave Sweden on the same commercial, but not political, footing as Denmark and Norway after their presumed accession. After Denmark's accession and Norway's rejection of the terms of accession in a national referendum, however, nothing more than a free trade treaty of the kind offered to backsliding Norway was on offer from the Community.

By the underlying circumstances of its creation at the outset of the Cold War the Community was not neutral. In Sweden, neutrality at the outset of the Cold War had popular approval.[22] Many Riksdag members who gave their consent to the Special Relations Agreement which was signed with the Community on 12 December 1972 might have been ready to support an agreement for full membership, but if this meant abandoning neutrality that number would have been reduced sufficiently to endanger Sweden's party and political stability.

Austrian neutrality had quite different origins. It was imposed by the State Treaty of 1955 which recreated an independent Austrian state. If the treaty was regarded as part of the overall European peace structure by both sides in the Cold War, Austria took a less fundamental view. Austrian political parties looked favourably on the growth of the European Communities in the 1950s and also, later, on the British proposal for a free trade area linked to the EEC, which might have given Austria the commercial advantages it sought without raising the issue of the State Treaty.[23] Neither was acceptable, it seemed, to the USSR, but Austria nevertheless pursued the idea of a neutral 'association' with the EEC. This, too, was regarded in Moscow as another *Ausgleich* with Germany and a breaking of the State Treaty. It was stalled as a way forward by de Gaulle's opposition to it, which may have had more in common with the Soviet Union's objections than he publicly declared, and then it was definitively killed in 1969 by the Italian government after Austrian irredentists carried out a terrorist bombing attack in the Alto Adige. Italy was not going to share a united Europe with a country which seemed still to harbour ideas from the 1930s. Like Sweden, Austria and Finland had to wait for the end of the Cold War before full EC/EU membership became possible.

The only neutral country which was allowed to enter the European Community before the German question was settled was Ireland, because its neutrality had nothing to do with the Cold War. There may well have been no country in Europe with so little business, diplomatic or economic, with and so much dislike of the Soviet Union. It was in protest against the partition of the island of Ireland that the Irish Republic stayed out of NATO. Its neutrality was a gesture against Britain. Its only value may have been as a substitute for ruminating over the failure of the Irish nationalist movement to convince the whole island of its cause. This was not a central issue for a threatened western Europe or, indeed, the USA. By the time of Ireland's application for accession to the Community, leading Irish politicians were only too ready to assure the leaders of the Six that they would not hesitate to take their part in the defence of the 'West', with which they wholly belonged and sympathised, should it be attacked. Nevertheless, they were asked for and had to provide for the first time an explanation, to France, of why Ireland was neutral. Ireland's negotiations for accession were almost wholly devoted to economic issues, but were, nevertheless, inseparable from the political hope of freeing the island from its political and economic domination by the United Kingdom.

It makes little sense therefore to argue that even the strongest economic motives were independent of or overrode major political considerations in the decision to join the EC/EU. The economic motives were strong for all countries seeking membership. While economic disputes have been fierce within the EC/EU, they have rarely called its existence into question. That cannot be said so confidently about the disputes over the extent of its political powers or even the lower order question of the nature of its political machinery. What the machinery and its powers should be in order to maintain its political objectives and ensure its continued economic strength and success has been a matter of almost permanently acrimonious dispute. If its objectives, economic and political, have held it together and attracted so many additional members, it may nevertheless be the case that no similarly successful international institution has had such heavily criticised and fiercely denounced political machinery.

There is little, if any, disagreement between political science and history about the political role which the first European Communities were intended to play. There has been much disagreement about the theoretical and practical reasons for the nature of their political machinery. If customs union theory with its clear propositions seems too narrow and mechanistic a tool for explaining why countries join the common market, political theory seems quite the opposite. Some of it explained forty years ago things that have not yet happened, nonetheless it tackles directly an issue which customs union theory skips blithely past, the possibility that the common market of the EU and any other customs union are too dissimilar to be embraced in one theory.

Other regional tariff unions do not require strings of meetings of national ministers and their officials for so wide a range of political activities. The arbitration rulings of other international trade organisations cannot compare with the history of legal judgements, an increasing amount of which is not obviously to do with commercial regulation, transacted by the European Court of Justice before being enforced, sometimes, on recalcitrant states. The EU has an almost daily political presence in the media of each member-state and much of that presence is not about commercial issues. The high level of political attention which the ECJ receives typically emphasises the issue of whither it is leading, of the political future facing the member-states. The common economic policies – agriculture, fisheries, and the common commercial policy – also receive a high frequency of attention in the national media. Some nation is always being 'cheated' or gaining 'unfair advantage' or is 'taking the lead' and the debate leaves commercial questions behind to focus on the political cockpit. To add to this catalogue, the EU has its own far-flung trade treaties with and provides aid to North and Sub-Saharan Africa and to Caribbean and Pacific economies. Most of these commercial relationships with the least developed economies spring from earlier western European political authority over the states in question and not infrequently there are still military and defence links.

The tendency of political science and history has been to see the sequential evolution of the politico-economic machinery of the European Communities as an answer to the problems of peaceful governance of a continent made up of a patchwork of rich and, in their recent history, belligerent states. The European Coal and Steel Community, for example, is seen by both disciplines as a solution to the post-Second World War problem of unifying and incorporating the American, British and French occupied zones of defeated Germany into 'the West' by creating the German Federal Republic as a western democratic state and rearming it. The first common market is thus accepted to have been born from high strategy out of the need to remobilise the damaged, partly sequestrated, partly dismantled German steel industry for rearmament under terms agreeable to the rest of western Europe. It was a device to place that birth under two favourable stars: the nearby one of a substitute political arrangement for a peace treaty, the distant one the hope of European political integration. The imaginative nature of the solution, with its occasionally visible rainbow of hope for an equally imaginative restructuring of the continent, appealed especially in contrast to the treaties which had brought so unpromising an end to the First World War.

The harsher aspects of the first Community, such as the breaking up of the ownership and cartel structure of the German steel industry, the changes imposed on its managerial structures, and the dissolution of the Ruhr Coal Cartel were not thought of as decisions carved for ever in stone, but as gauges of a democratic Germany's commitment to the substitute peace. Once they had served their political purpose, there was a tacit, and even in some cases a collusive, acceptance of a second reconstruction, re-establishing much of the former ownership pattern of steelworks and coalmines in the Federal Republic. There is a substantial body of historical research which has increasingly authenticated this instrumental interpretation of the 'deconstruction' and the 'reconstruction' of the German steel industry.[24] Not only was the supranational High Authority of the Coal and Steel Community subordinate to the major political interests of its member-states, but it had little or no influence on their policies. It was merely a channel through which national policies flowed. Nevertheless, this literature, whether conceived as political theory or history, does not regard the symbolism of the High Authority and the ECSC as hollow. It emphasises its importance to the achievement of the political goals of the participants. There was very little supranational governance emanating from the ECSC, but the existence of the supranational institution in itself was essential to what was achieved.

From that point onward political science and history diverge into two schools of political interpretation of European integration. One springs from the various federalist political movements in Europe, some of which had drafted constitutions and manifestoes hoping to create some kind of united movement to establish a single federal government for the democratic part of the continent. The other is influenced by varieties of 'functional' political theory, deriving from efforts in the 1930s to establish a more effective form of politics which sought rational solutions to particular problems rather than proposing general styles and codes of political behaviour, democracy for example, as requisites demanded by history. Functionalists and federalists joined in the hope that, with the overthrow of the Nazi regime, European politics would swing in the direction of a less emotional, less brutal, less wasteful and more rational form of government. Functionalists laid the foundation for the political science of European integration, not paying much regard as they did so to the economic properties of customs unions.

Theory appeals to those who want the outcome which the theory predicts. Both federalists and functionalists believed that the politics they supported would triumph because of their innately greater rationality and both were thus prone to exaggerate the rationality, the federal promise and the rational functionalism of the political machinery of the ECSC. Advocates of federal government saw it as a way of bringing national government closer to the people as well as of better equilibrating the interests of different linguistic, ethnic or economic interests within the state and within Europe. Their hopes were understandably high that after the events of 1939–45 the necessity for such equilibration at a supranational level might be more evident. The all-too-evident inability of the nation-states in the inter-war period to cope with the difficulties they faced led too easily to the conclusion that European integration was a reflection of the growing persuasiveness of federalist politics.

There was never much clarity about what federalism at a continental level would truly be for. Transcendence of the innately warlike motives which permeated the structure of the centralised state was perhaps believable as a possibility, although faced by Soviet belligerence western European states needed to prepare for war. A stronger claim for constitutional change and European unity was more usually connected to the advocacy of written constitutions. The perfection of political practice in equilibrating interests which might, if not equilibrated, lead to political fragmentation or to an authoritarian centralisation of government typically depended on belief in the strength of the written word and its underpinning by law. In the light of the events of the 1930s this lacked a certain credibility. Federalists were not able to identify a sufficiently substantial programme of what a European federal state would actually do, rather than uphold as a principle. Their concentration on constitutional change failed to apply itself to the practical resolution of the social and economic problems of definable scope common to almost every western European state in post-war reconstruction: a severely damaged infrastructure, the lack of an effective international trade and payments mechanism, hunger, poverty and social disruption.

The will to tackle these problems on a continental scale was more evident in the development of functionalist politics, whose advocates in the inter-war period had argued for a politics which aimed at rational solutions to targeted problems common to most states and requiring a solution which transcended national boundaries. Federalists could applaud as their own some aspects of ECSC. Functionalists could applaud its creation outside the framework of traditional international relations and its supranational focus on resolving a major economic problem by transnational economic and social policies. To functionalists it seemed to confirm the correctness of their arguments in the inter-war period in favour of finding technical solutions of limited but common problems.

For both functionalists and federalists the pre-1939 European nation-state had shown itself inadequate as a political machine. Federalists could claim that to the problem of concentrating political attention and resources on problems of definable scope it was they who had the constitutional answer. But when it came to the prioritisation of human needs and public welfare after 1945 the centralised state turned out to be well able to rebuild itself by pursuing functionalist policies. Even if in pursuing functionalist politics its fiscal authority and its budgetary power were less sensitively focused than might have been the case under a federalist constitution, the contrasting political reality of the ECSC, powerless as it was in the hands of its nation-state creators, was not such as to make a strong case for European federalism.

From the study of the ECSC at work a neo-functionalist school of political science did at first claim that this was successful functionalism in practice, a model which could be copied, although the leader of the school had renounced that view by 1968.[25] The functional problem which had required solving was the distribution of a scarce resource, coal and coke, between the rival national producers of steel. The High Authority of the ECSC, whose members had pledged themselves not to support their own national interest, were seen as pioneers in international functional problem-solving. Where the nation had deceived functionalist hopes of a more rational and efficient political process, the new 'supranation' was now identified as the political form which would realise them. The main scholarly architects of this identification, Ernst Haas and Leon Lindberg, were not, however, merely identifying functionalist hopes of the 1930s with political actualities of the 1950s and 1960s; they were seeking to explain the political process of European integration and in doing so building a theory of integration from the working of the first European Community institutions. The theory they generated, and which Haas later criticised and modified, provided an explanation of why in the future other countries would join the Communities. No other political theory of Community expansion was to hold the field for so long as the functionalist explanation of why states would join a customs union with a common political system. It became the counterpart in political science of customs union theory in economics and an alternative teleology to it.

In elaborating this body of theory Haas and Lindberg were in fact some way from the attitudes, and what seem also to have been the assumptions, of earlier functionalists. They did not suppose that this new supranational functionalism had arisen because of its irrefutable superiority as a form of governance. They explained the development as the consequence of the political activity of interest groups and influential politicians; politics in the pursuit of self-interest was generating integration. The drift of the argument was that self-interest pursued through pluralist politics in pluralist societies would generate integration, sometimes even for unplanned or accidental reasons. Integration came via the need for some political machinery that targeted functional problems, through the accidental conjunction of this with the security requirement that western Europe act together, through the activities of certain leading figures such as Jean Monnet or Paul-Henri Spaak, but also because once some organisation like the ECSC was set up to solve a functional problem and was staffed by government functionaries, those functionaries would see themselves as peculiarly well-placed to cooperate with their counterparts from other nations in finding functional solutions to other problems. It was not only that they might group behind the best solution, irrespective of their own nation's policy, but, more importantly, would look for solutions within a transnational rather than a national form. Even David

Mitrany, the most persistent advocate of functionalist politics, to the point where he thought regional transnational institutions were a harmful circumscription of the power of functionalism, argued that through the new institutions of ECSC, Euratom and the EEC a notable step forward in the development of a functional politics of Europe had been achieved.[26]

The neo-functionalist account of the first three European Communities – ECSC, EEC and Euratom – supposed that there was an inherent tendency in the new supranational political machinery which would lead it to extend its activities to the functionalist solution of other problems within the same supranational or transnational framework. Haas and Lindberg both argued that strengthening the integrationist ties in one sector of the economy, 'deepening', would lead to the search for integration in other sectors affected by that strengthening, an argument on which, as we have noted, Baldwin also relied. As that happened, more power would shift to the supranational agencies. A customs union would lead to exchange rate stabilisation, exchange rate stabilisation to coordination of monetary policy, coordination of monetary policy to a monetary union. Larger political consequences would follow from a limited forward step in integration. 'Spillover' became the essential explanatory mechanism of European integration.

A theory which rested on the political processes of pluralistic democracies of all kinds, rather than on claims for the innate superiority of one form of governance over others, carried more conviction, the more so because its proponents incorporated into their descriptions of its operations the notion that pluralist politics was an uncertain and messy affair with outcomes that were sometimes accidental. They also related somewhat haphazard political processes to new international political forms of organisation, explaining something of the origins of those organisations and of the growing need for them in the post-war world.

Unfortunately, the ingenuity of neo-functionalist theory did not, as historians were to show, rest on an observable, factual foundation. European nations created the institutions of integration to pursue national agendas. They kept too tight a rein and too close a supervisory control over the institutions for functionalist policies to emerge independently through the interplay of their own functionaries dispatched to serve in those institutions. The states internationalised or transnationalised their policies only when it was easier, or absolutely necessary, to do so. The new institutions of integration only represented the birth of a new politics of the future in the sense that state policies covered a wider range of social and economic activities than before 1939, had more similarities than before 1939, and in certain cases were thus more likely to be successful if pursued through the supranational structure. 'Spillover', like Europeanising its policies, remained something that the state could still choose or reject. Similarly, it could reject any policies emerging from within the supranational political framework itself. The essential task for theory was to understand why particular policies were pursued through the supranational institutions and others not. To do that it must still have the state as its main focus.[27]

This reasoning from historical evidence did not by any means weaken the case for a theory of the relationship of the institutions of European integration to the decision of states to join the European Communities, nor for a theory of more limited scope about the role the Community institutions were likely to play in that process. It merely observed that the Communities did not expand because of their inherent tendency to generate functionalist policies. They could expand only through decisions made at state level. Historical work took the empirical path of showing the complex origins of those policies which were Europeanised in order to reach some clearer statements about why states did choose to pursue some policies through Community institutions.[28]

Historical research is more restricted temporally than are theoretical propositions. The most liberal of national governments open their archives to inspection by the public only between twenty-five or thirty years after the events they deal with. A historical analysis of the functioning of the European state in 1972 may well not tell much about the relationship of the functioning of the European state in 2004 to the European Union. Even so, neo-functionalist predictions that 'spillover' would lead to Community expansion showed a remarkable blindness to the function which the EEC mainly undertook, trade regulation and trade negotiation. The political machinery of the European Communities mattered far more, it seemed, for the future than what so many of its functionaries were dealing with in the present.

There were other schools of political science offering different explanations for the supranational institutions of the 1950s. Deutsch, for example, saw them as a part of the proliferation of international institutions at the time, and saw that proliferation in turn as a measure of the increase in 'transactions' between democratic states, especially in the 'West'.[29] Under transactions he listed everything from pan-European football competitions to the common market, by way of town-twinning between local authorities and the internationalising activities of academics and tourists. This, too, showed a certain indifference to foreign trade, which nineteenth century internationalists had thought of as the best route to 'the Parliament of Man, the Federation of the World'. It might have been thought that trade liberalisation was the best route also to wealth generation, but political science seemed uninterested in demonstrations by historians and economists that the rapid evolution in the structural pattern of foreign trade between the western European states was a powerful stimulus to further integration by means of trade, in spite of the unwillingness of politicians to leave such vital matters for decision to technocratic functionaries meeting away from their national capitals.

It is not surprising therefore that when Moravcsik, writing within the paradigms of political science, also brought historical research to his aid to bolster and refine a historical argument that integration and its institutions were in fact a means by which the nation-state strengthened itself, his work was received by historians more sympathetically and with less criticism than by political scientists.[30] Detailed historical research had supported neither the teleological implications of customs union theory nor those of neo-functionalism. Indeed, on the basis of the historical evidence it could be more plausibly argued that the expansion of the European Communities was not attributable to any long-term economic or political forces, but was, rather, a series of stochastic events, each separate expansion requiring its own historical explanation. Nevertheless, some continuity was provided by the nation-state's use of the supranational integrationist institutions to strengthen and secure policy choices which had been taken domestically. Moravcsik developed more deeply the concept that the integrationist machinery of the EEC/EU permitted any member-states to play a two-level game in which domestic political actors working within the bounds of rational choice theory could pursue policy choices, some of which emerged as national preferences which were then bargained for intergovernmentally at the supranational institutional level. It should be noted that tariff and trade bargaining being a prime example of this two-level game activity in the mid-nineteenth century, to which Moravcsik's own description of the process as 'liberal intergovernmentalism' surely did not have only accidental reference, one advantage of his rephrasing the historical research which had laid the ground for him was that he focused political science on the EEC's main activity, trade and its regulation.

In arguing his case Moravcsik gave scant consideration to the supra-national symbolism of the international venue where the second stage of the game is played. Is the EU in reality no more than an intergovernmental institution? Even if its political role as the unifier of Europe is rarely fruitful and scarcely pursuable, given the attitude of its member-states, it nevertheless has to be taken into account in the way the 'game' is played. Could a merely intergovernmental institution coexist with the European Court of Justice, which can and does reject and amend national legislation as it can also overturn decisions of the European Commission? And, to bring the discussion back to the central theme of the chapter, may not the arena in which the two-level game has to be played give rise to some integrative momentum? The policies which reach the Committee of Permanent Representatives (Corepers) and Council of Ministers of the EU perhaps bear testimony to an increasing institutionalisation of supranational decision-making. The very process of playing a two-level game in the EU arena means that some member-state is always pleading the case of a policy that tallies more closely with what may be the European Commission's own political agenda. If, furthermore, the nature of the European nation-state is changing with increased liberalisation, if liberalisation and globalisation erode its centralised structure, then what Moravcsik sees as the resolute and rational pursuit of intergovernmental bargaining over traditional issues, albeit in a more internationalised setting, may be a reflection of the necessary and ongoing adaptation of the state to the changed international circumstances.[31] Outsiders can never be sure that it is not their interests which insider Corepers and Councils of Ministers are discussing.

Teleologies, political and economic, sprout like Hydra's heads. Customs union theory persistently hypothesises that customs unions have an inherent and increasingly powerful leverage over those states that remain outside, a leverage made up of increasing potential gains foregone and increasing penalties paid. Political theory searches restlessly for a way of better explaining the tendency of states in Europe to surrender elements of national sovereignty. In marking exceptions history does not necessarily invalidate general theories about why European states have formed a European Union with such complicated and disputed political institutions, while it underlines the powerful attraction of a customs union in the area of the globe that has more contiguous, high-per-capita-income economies, all of them highly dependent on international trade, jostling together than any other. That each member-state strikes its own deal with the EC/EU, while accepting the *acquis communautaire*, shows how carefully considered the sovereignty surrenders are. Even more so does the calculated choice of specific important national politico-economic objectives within the Community. Both show that the concept of the nation survived the tidal wave of adjustment to the necessities of post-war political and economic adjustment in Europe. No earlier European institution was joined by so many states, paying the price for the peace which has brought the economic benefits they have reaped. Retaining the concept of a national political economy has been, so far, a way of reducing that price. Adjustment will always be necessary, as in all systems of international relations. In which direction is not safely predictable.

2 Denmark, Ireland and the political economy of industrialisation

The original six members of the European Economic Community were developed industrial economies. The common market which they created was a market for an increasing and also an increasingly liberalised trade in sophisticated manufactured goods. This trade between them had grown rapidly and powerfully from the earliest years of western Europe's post-war reconstruction, so that the structure and pattern of trade within the common market existed already before the Treaty of Rome brought it formally into existence and accelerated the existing interchange of manufactured products between its signatories. Of that interchange the German Federal Republic was the pivot, before and after the birth of the EEC, the most important supplier of capital goods to the other member-states and also the biggest and most rapidly growing market for exports of machinery, chemicals and most other manufactures within the common market. The volume of this interchange was such as to industrialise in the 1950s most of those areas of western Europe which had remained unindustrialised, or relatively so, before 1945. When the great post-war European industrialisation boom came to its end in 1972 this pattern of trade did not alter, although its value and volume grew less consistently and less rapidly. Germany remained the pivot of the system and the United Kingdom after its entry in that year slotted, after initial difficulties, into the role of another, but smaller, Germany.

Table 2.1 shows how large the share of the German Federal Republic remained in the intra-trade within the common market in engineering products (SITC 7). German exports of machinery were always more than one-third of total engineering exports between common market members until the disruptions of the early 1990s when the German share declined. After 1995 it recovered strongly. If we exclude road vehicles from the calculation the German share was larger before 1990 but much smaller after 1990. Cars, being an assembly of engineering products made in almost all common market states, are the archetypal case of a final product whose manufacture depends on intra-trade. The tendency of the German automobile

Table 2.1 Share of German Federal Republic exports in EC/EU intra-trade in engineering products (SITC 7) (current values)

	All engineering products (%)	Excluding road vehicles (%)
1963	35.1	46.5
1970	44.1	46.4
First expansion		
1975	36.2	30.9
1980	36.8	39.2
1985	34.7	39.7
Second expansion		
1990	34.5	33.4
Third expansion		
1995	20.8	11.9
2000	26.8	13.3

Source: Eurostat, *External Trade, Statistical Yearbooks*, passim.

firms to shift car assembly to lower wage countries is probably an important factor underlying the greater statistical difference which appears in the 1990s if road vehicles are excluded from the calculation.

In comparison the British share of intra-trade in the same products varied from between one-third of the German share to one-half (Table 2.2). After 1975 the share is slightly larger when road vehicles are excluded. United States sales of the same products (SITC 7) inside the common market were more important as a fraction of total German sales than were British, reflecting the USA's position as the world's biggest supplier of capital goods. From 1970 onwards, however, the American share of the market was steadily, if slowly, declining, to rise very steeply and suddenly after 1995 (Table 2.3). Japan became an important competitor only in the 1970s. In that decade its sales of engineering products inside the common market rose from 7.7 per cent of Germany's sales (in 1970) to 28.7 per cent in 1980, before settling at around 40 per cent from 1985 onwards (Table 2.3). With tariff reductions, therefore, both Japan and the USA had a large market in the EEC but even their presence on such a scale did not displace Germany from its central role in the intra-trade in capital goods.

The European Community's first expansion took place at the point where the post-war rate of growth of output in western Europe slowed down and for the first time since 1945 strong cyclical economic fluctuations returned. It was not therefore the most opportune moment to be joining for Britain nor for Denmark and Ireland, for both of which industrialisation had become an important domestic objective and prominent among their motives for seeking membership.

Industrialisation had been an objective of the Irish government in the 1930s, pursued in the international pattern of that decade of deploying highly

Table 2.2 UK share of exports in EC/EU intra-trade in capital goods and road vehicles (SITC 7) (current values)

	All engineering products (%)	Engineering products excluding road vehicles (%)
(1963)	(14.8)	(14.3)
(1970)	(11.7)	(n.a.)
	UK entry	
1975	12.0	16.6
1980	14.3	17.4
1985	12.9	17.7
1990	12.9	15.6
1995	11.6	13.9
2000	13.3	14.8

Source: Eurostat, *External Trade*, *Statistical Yearbooks*, passim.

Table 2.3 USA and Japanese sales of engineering products (SITC 7) inside EC/EU as proportion of German sales (current values)

	USA (%)	Japan (%)
1963	44.1	2.05
1970	52.7	7.70
1975	51.1	19.5
1980	50.0	28.7
1985	43.4	40.0
1990	43.3	38.9
1995	39.9	38.1
2000	61.1	39.7

Source: Eurostat, *External Trade*, *Statistical Yearbooks*, passim.

protectionist tariffs as the way forward. Unsuccessful then, except in so far as it attracted some British firms to open subsidiaries in Ireland to supply the Irish market, its inadequacy became more marked as trade liberalisation took hold throughout western Europe from 1956 onwards. In Denmark, a greater level of industrialisation was the policy of the first post-war Social Democratic government, which sought unavailingly to use Marshall Plan funding to back such a programme. The coalition governments that followed were not committed to the same extent. The Danish industrial sector remained highly protected while agricultural exports remained the main foreign exchange earner. Persistent balance of payments deficits in the 1950s emphasised the weakness of this position but also meant that capital for investment in the industrial sector was scarce. The liberalisation of trade in the 1950s did not touch agricultural trade which remained tightly regulated and controlled by government. Danish agriculture, whose exports had been in previous times the most powerful stimulus to the growth of the economy, waited in vain for an opening in which its competitive advantages could be deployed.

There is an economic similarity between the post-war experiences of the three states, Denmark, Ireland and the United Kingdom, which entered the European Community on 1 January 1972. They were three of the four most slowly growing economies in post-war western Europe. The other was Belgium, already a member of the EEC. The average annual percentage increase in GDP of all OEEC countries over the period 1953–61 was 4.9 per cent. In the same period the figure for Denmark was 3.9 per cent, for the United Kingdom 2.9 per cent and for Ireland 1.8 per cent. In the period 1961–73 (when they had become OECD countries) Denmark and Ireland did better, Ireland in particular showing a rapid acceleration in growth, although both still grew more slowly than the average for European OECD member-states. The OECD average was 4.7 per cent annually. Denmark and Ireland recorded an annual average increase of 4.3 per cent. In the same decade the United Kingdom earned its title as the sick man of Europe with an annual average growth of GDP of only 3.1 per cent, the lowest in western Europe. The significance of these comparisons is strengthened by the fact that the fourth applicant for accession, Norway, performed only marginally better than its three fellow applicants, recording an average annual percentage increase of GDP over the period 1953–61 of 3.4 per cent and in 1961–73 of 4.3 per cent. All other countries except Sweden surpassed the average for OECD Europe over those decades.[1] The first applicants for accession to the EEC were therefore the weakest economic performers of those eligible, assuming Sweden to be ineligible because of its preference for internationally recognised neutrality.

The United Kingdom's relatively low growth rate over a period character-ised elsewhere in Europe by persistently high growth rates raises the question whether there is not a further similarity between the three smaller applicants: the extent of their trade dependence on the slow-growing United Kingdom. While Britain remained throughout the first two post-war decades a major market for all three of its fellow applicants, the differences between the three countries in the dimensions of their trade relationships with the United Kingdom over those twenty years are too great to allow any conclusion other than the obvious one that the rate of growth of imports into a slower growing country is likely to be more sluggish than into a faster growing country.

Yet even this conclusion does not offer any sound basis for saying that slow growth of national income in Britain held back rates of economic growth in Denmark, Ireland and Norway. The fastest-growing country, Germany, was an important market for Norway and until 1967 was the second-biggest market for Denmark. Furthermore, it is inappropriate, as Table 2.4 shows, to equate the degree of trade dependence on the British market of the two Scandinavian countries with that of Ireland. Denmark and Norway each sold in the 1950s about a quarter of the total value of their exports to the United Kingdom.[2] Table 2.4 shows that this proportion diminished significantly in the 1960s. Ireland, however, was selling three-quarters of its total exports by value to Britain in 1960 and two-thirds in 1970. A highly trade-dependent economy, it had in effect only one large market.

In 1960 agricultural exports (SITC 0) made up only marginally less than a half of the total value of both Danish and Irish exports (Table 2.5). That large share still meant that less than 40 per cent of Danish agricultural exports had Britain as their destination.[3] Germany was also a large market. A rich agricultural exporter, Denmark could continue to concentrate its primary exports on the British market, because it had a substantial agricultural market in Germany also and other markets for raw materials, primary and manufactured goods. Ireland, with a lower standard of living, had no other worthwhile

Table 2.4 Exports to the United Kingdom as a percentage of total exports

	1960	*1965*	*1970*
Denmark	26.30	22.31	18.92
Ireland	74.89	70.62	66.30
Norway	22.61	17.79	17.92

Source: OECD, Department of Economics and Statistics, *Foreign Trade by Commodities*, annual volumes.

Table 2.5 Denmark and Ireland as agricultural exporters to the United Kingdom, 1960–70

	Agricultural products (SITC 0) as % of total exports		*Agricultural products to the UK as % of total exports to the UK*		*Agricultural products to the UK as % of total agricultural exports*	
	Denmark	*Ireland*	*Denmark*	*Ireland*	*Denmark*	*Ireland*
1960	54.80	54.09	88.48	59.03	42.48	81.72
1965	46.35	55.07	81.02	60.62	38.99	77.73
1970	33.83	45.48	65.18	52.48	36.45	81.73

Source: OECD, Department of Economics and Statistics, *Foreign Trade by Commodities*, annual volumes.

market either for agricultural or manufactured exports. This reflected propinquity and the long earlier existence of Britain and Ireland as a political union. What was a matter of choice for Denmark was a matter of compulsion for Ireland; its exporters had no other outlet. Both were dependent on import prices fixed by the British government, but Denmark had more bargaining leverage, notably so when Britain needed its support for the free trade area proposal and then in the formation of EFTA. The political factor helps to explain why, throughout the decade 1960–70, agricultural products were so much higher a proportion of its exports to the United Kingdom than they were of Irish exports to the same destination (Table 2.5).

As the same table shows, however, it was only after 1965 that industrialisation brought about a decisive shift in the commodity structure of Ireland's foreign trade. This was related to the change in Irish–British trade relations that came with the Anglo-Irish Free Trade Area Agreement signed towards the end of that year. This agreement was itself a response to centrally formulated national development plans in Ireland intended to give a more outward-looking orientation to the economy by reducing tariff protection and linking government to the direction of domestic industrial investment. This important change in the nature of industrialisation policy came after 1958 as a response to the formation of the common market.[4] Denmark's industrialisation over the same period was a more gradual and less volatile process, starting in 1945 from an already more developed, although heavily protected, manufacturing sector. For both, however, industrialisation policy was a response to shifts in the international trading framework during the 1950s and to the difficulties of managing the balance of payments when export earnings were so dependent on agricultural produce. The arrangements made by the larger west European economies to liberalise intra-European trade in manufactures while leaving agricultural trade to be closely managed by government played a large part in prompting government intervention in industrial investment policy, but the combination of post-war recovery policy and Keynesian economics were also favourable towards government 'planning' throughout western Europe.

The mutual exceptionalism of Denmark and Ireland after 1945 is that, in response to this pressure, and with the exception of what would now be called 'mini-states', they were the only two western European economies for which the German Federal Republic did not become the main market for their manufactured exports and the main supplier of their capital goods imports. The two European Community member-states which entered the common market on 1 January 1973 in the pursuit of industrialisation thus did not follow the pattern of the first member-states, nor of later member-states, and rely on an increasing interchange of manufactures with Germany to drive industrialisation forwards.

Denmark, furthermore, did not have an export trade in manufactures with the United Kingdom which reflected either the importance of the UK as Europe's second biggest importer of manufactures or the weight of manufacturing in the Danish economy. It needs explanation that a country whose disposable national income per capita in 1960–1 was somewhere between 15 and 20 per cent higher than that of the United Kingdom, whose manufacturing labour force was more than four times greater than employment in agriculture, where agriculture accounted for only 18 per cent of national product and manufacturing more than one quarter, should have had four-fifths of its exports to Britain made up of food and fodder.[5]

Historical reasons can be found. The Danish economy had grown rapidly in the three decades before the First World War through agricultural exports to free trade Britain. It had done so on the basis of products tailored to the British market, bacon and butter in particular. In the inter-war recession, and even through the Great Depression of 1929–33, this export trade, before and after the United Kingdom's return to tariff protection, had stood up well. Denmark was one of the few large-scale food exporters which survived the inter-war problems almost unscathed. Danish agriculture was highly capitalised and much of its export output was processed. Bacon still accounted in 1960, together with pigs, for more than one-third of the total value of Danish agricultural exports to Britain. The second most valuable category was butter, which also through packaging, standardised consistency, branding and quality had conquered a large market there in the inter-war years.

Competition – Ireland was a competitor – was greatly limited by import quotas and bilateral treaties.[6] But if the persistence of controlled trade in Britain helps to explain the high share of agricultural exports in Denmark's trade with the UK, it cannot after 1956 be the reason for the low presence of Danish manufactures on the British market. British imports of Danish machinery (SITC 7), the most rapidly growing sector of world trade in manufactures, were only 42 per cent of the value of similar Danish exports to Sweden and 40 per cent of those to Germany in 1960. Norway, too, was a much larger market for Danish machinery than Britain, Finland a market of almost the same size. Danish machinery exports to Britain in 1958 were of almost the same value as exports of bacon and pigs. Each made up 14 per cent of the total value.[7]

In his classic study of trade in manufactures between industrialised economies before 1960 Maizels found neither Denmark nor Ireland worthy of consideration.[8] If EFTA did not by its existence change the commodity structure of Danish–British trade there was no good reason why the common market should do so after 1972. A trio of Scandinavian states, Sweden, Norway and Finland, remained the dominant market for Danish manufactured exports. Sweden remained a more important single market than Britain or

Germany. For Ireland, the opposite was the case; the United Kingdom remained Ireland's biggest market for manufactured exports and in that respect was a major contributor to Ireland's industrialisation. Why did Denmark's industrialisation continue within an intra-Scandinavian pattern of industrial exchange and in doing so sacrifice the advantages of increased interchange with Germany and even the lesser advantages of intra-trade in manufactures with the United Kingdom?

A comparison of the foreign trade of Denmark and Ireland has been made, not by any Danish or Irish author, but by the Norwegian social scientist Lars Mjøset in a report produced by the Institute for Social Research in Oslo for the National Economic and Social Council of Ireland.[9] In a wide-ranging study the concern of Mjøset and his team was to uncover the institutional factors in Ireland's rapid economic development. The report did not confine itself to institutional history of a narrowly administrative kind. It regarded markets as a subject of institutional enquiry, a justified perspective in the case of post-war international trade in agricultural products. Farmers and landowners' associations as well as government-sponsored marketing boards and cooperatives played an active and persistent role in their management. The liberalisation of non-agricultural trade altered only the more remote international institutional frameworks of association. The main instrument of management remained import quotas, whether negotiated between governments and paid for within bilateral agreements or negotiated by governments within the European Community framework and the payments settled between governments and the European Commission. For Denmark and Ireland these institutionalised markets were at first regulated directly between governments, even after Denmark had entered EFTA, and from the start of 1973 within the European Community. Why did both countries make the choice to join the common market?

In so far as there was any economic interest in either country in the European Communities in the first decade after 1958 it came from farmers, in the Danish case from the larger landowners and particularly their representation in Venstre. In both countries farmers' interest in the EC was stimulated by the low prices which prevailed for agricultural products on British markets.

The only other large market for agricultural imports was Germany, but for Denmark it was no alternative to the British market. The most valuable item in Denmark's agricultural exports to Germany was cattle transported across the border for feeding and eventual slaughtering. Comparable British imports of cattle came from Ireland. In Germany Irish farmers had no more than a toehold, mainly for meat. High German prices had no effect on British prices. Free entry for Commonwealth food exports, arriving in British ports more cheaply than European food and not subject in most instances to a tariff, kept down the prices paid for supply from Ireland and the continent. Ireland enjoyed the same preferences as Commonwealth countries, but preferences, even free entry, did not improve prices. Irish farmers correctly assumed that food prices under the EEC's Common Agricultural Policy would be much higher than in the UK. When the British government first began in 1960 seriously considering an application to join the EEC, its initial assumption about domestic food prices was that they might rise by as much as 7.5 per cent as soon as Britain was inside the Community. British farmers did not receive Irish or Danish prices for their produce. They were subsidised by the state paying them directly for the difference between the retail price of their produce to the consumer and a figure supposed to represent its higher production cost. Danish and Irish farmers received prices based closely on the desired retail price in Britain. They could hardly fail to observe that the higher sums which British farmers received would, by stimulating higher output, gradually reduce their own market in the UK.

While smaller farmers in both Ireland and Denmark had their well-justified fears that the big rewards of the CAP might be reaped by farmers on a grander scale, these were counterbalanced by the precariousness of dependence on one market in a country where the seemingly inevitable tendency of domestic agricultural policy would be to generate more domestic supply and even in some products surpluses. The attractive aspects of the CAP's objectives as set out in the vague clauses of the Treaty of Rome were that such problems would be managed on a European scale and not in bilateral bargaining with a far more powerful trade partner and that they would be managed within an economic universe of higher returns to farmers. For Danish agriculture it was, additionally, obvious that the situation would be easier if the United Kingdom and Germany were in the same trading bloc and the United Kingdom governed by the rules of the CAP.

Agricultural interest group pressure could be brought to bear on the Folketing, the Danish parliament, through Venstre. For Danish industrial interests, however, EFTA had to be the correct choice, because their two biggest markets, Sweden and Norway, were EFTA members. Agricultural trade was not included in EFTA's tariff-cutting programmes. Before joining, however, Denmark forced an agreement from Britain which included a provision for the complete removal over the two years 1960–1 of all duties on Danish bacon and canned pork luncheon meat as well as the immediate abolition of the British tariffs on Danish blue-veined cheese and tinned cream. It was the one breach in the principle that any trading arrangements made with European economies must avoid eliminating preferences enjoyed by Commonwealth countries on the British market. That had been one British reason for insisting on a free trade area rather than some form of customs union. It was therefore in British eyes a large concession, but a necessary one to swing Danish agriculture into line with the Danish manufacturers' interest in joining EFTA.

Unavoidable though Denmark's choice of EFTA was on economic grounds, Venstre and Danish agriculture showed a persistent level of interest in the EEC as an economic and, increasingly, as a political choice. The parliamentary group of Venstre recommended Danish membership of the EEC in 1957, a recommendation followed by the party in June 1958. The party, however, changed its mind in November under the persuasion that the United Kingdom and EFTA would be closely linked to the EEC once within the free trade area, a serious misjudgement of French foreign policy. There were internal divisions over the question inside the party, for its liberal persuasions did not fit well with the battery of EEC interventionist arrangements. Venstre's interest in the terms on which Denmark might be admitted to the EEC nevertheless persisted.[10] Their dilemma was resolved by the United Kingdom's decision in 1961 to apply for membership of the Communities and reopened in 1963 by the French veto on British entry.

The Irish farmers' outlook on the EEC was determined by their geographical circumstances. It was telescopic. They looked through and beyond the United Kingdom to a distant continent. A long pursuit of better market terms in Britain was but a path from which they glimpsed a continental market which, although it might not be so large, offered the safety of regulation by a body in which they would have some say, higher prices for their output and a life less fraught by the task of perpetual bargaining with an overweening neighbour. Irish governments looked at a similar view, but more hesitantly. They had an industrial sector to consider, small, heavily protected by tariffs and with its market overwhelmingly in the United Kingdom where, in common with many Commonwealth countries, many of its manufactured exports had received duty-free entry. Irish protectionism as western Europe moved towards trade liberalisation was defended as buying time while industries developed behind the tariff barrier. The defence was only possible so long as British commercial policy did not change. The British free trade area proposal would have destroyed what validity there was in Irish industrialisation policy. Leisurely though the timetable for reaching a European Free Trade Area was, it was not leisurely enough to meet Ireland's wishes. In any case, whether Ireland joined or not, the preferential aspect of its duty-free entry for manufactured exports to Britain would be lost, while agricultural exports would not gain because agricultural trade was excluded from the proposed arrangements.

With its response undecided, Ireland secured the chairmanship in the negotiations of OEEC Working Party No. 17, whose function was to look at the problems of less-developed economies within the proposed free trade area, something on which Portugal was strongly insisting. One reason for

Portugal's insistence was to bring pressure on Britain to include agricultural trade within the proposal. There was already strong pressure in that direction from Denmark. It was feared in Dublin that Denmark would demand a price for joining the free trade area and that this might be the enlargement of quotas for imports into Britain of Danish bacon, butter and eggs. Even Ireland's agricultural exports were thus under threat.

Irish reactions to this impending rearrangement of commercial rules sheds an interesting light on the simplified assumptions from customs union theory. The European Free Trade Area proposal was certainly an idiosyncratic shock for Dublin. It was in fact the shock which ultimately led to a fundamental change of policy. But Ireland's reactions to it were the opposite for some time of theoretical predictions. The Department of Industry and Commerce predicted that to join the free trade area would mean a decline of more than one-third in the value of Irish exports to the United Kingdom.[11] Ireland lent no support to Danish and Portuguese requests for agricultural trade to be included in the proposal. 'The deliberations of the Six', so the Department of Agriculture reported to the government, 'have shown that if agriculture is to be included in a free trade area it would be preferable that this should be done on the basis of a common market under which essential safeguards such as harmonisation of agricultural policies, market organisation, etc, could be extended to meet the special problems of farmers.'[12] If Ireland could not envisage industrial competition within a free trade area whose schedules for tariff removal in its early discussions seemed as though they would be more leisurely than those of the EEC, it had to be asked what sort of a 'Common Market' Ireland's Department of Agriculture envisaged. The only possible answer seems to be 'between ourselves and Britain',[13] as the Department of Agriculture indeed suggested.

The reasoning behind the policy not to press for the inclusion of agricultural trade as an integral aspect of the European Free Trade Area was not confined to the conclusion that to exclude it would be less damaging to Irish exports to Britain than to include it, but also based on the assumption that the British industrial economy would grow more rapidly inside such a free trade area. The consequence would be a growth in the value of Irish agricultural exports to Britain. This could be assured if the necessary arrangements could be made between the two governments.

This conclusion side-stepped the problem of the future of Ireland's industrial sector. It was consulted, but there was not time to wait for all the answers before the meeting in early February 1957 of the OEEC Council at which Ireland had to take up a position. The advice given to the government by officials of the Department of Industry and Commerce was that a large part of Ireland's existing industry could not survive even as suppliers to the domestic market without permanent protection and that there was no prospect of a significant expansion of manufactured exports from Ireland to the continent if it became a member of the proposed European Free Trade Area. Staying out of the free trade area would mean increasing isolation within OEEC and perhaps the end of all hopes of increasing Ireland's exports to the continent. Furthermore, it would only increase the economic differences between the Irish Republic and Northern Ireland. The way forward, if such it was, recommended to ministers was to take no decision about the free trade area until the extent of the safeguards which would be granted to less-developed member-states had been discovered.

Caution was understandable, but offered no real way of making Irish membership of the free trade area possible, as Ireland's eventual decision not to join EFTA confirmed. The only alternative appeared to be some form of closer bilateral trading relationship with the United Kingdom. If the outcome was to be economic reintegration with the United Kingdom, it would, the Department of Finance noted, 'be a sad commentary on our industrial and agricultural policy over the past thirty years.'[14] That could not be gainsaid. The policy of a permanent protection of Irish manufacturing made no sense for a small country with no tariff bargaining power in a continent moving rapidly towards tariff elimination. It was in these circumstances, however, that the proposal to link a free trade area to the European Economic Community's common market, the proposal terminated by a French veto in November 1958, was in fact to prove fruitful in Ireland. It led to an urgent and comprehensive review of Irish economic development policy, from which was to be born a more effective industrialisation programme, albeit that the birth was long drawn out.

If the alternative to membership in a free trade area was a closer economic relationship with the United Kingdom, then, as the Department of Agriculture noted in the free trade area discussions,

> At this point the question arises whether, if we were to have unrestricted competition from British industrial exports under a free trade area, we should not have it in the form of a common market (on the lines of Benelux) between ourselves and Britain, and obtain the advantages of joint market organisation, harmonisation of agricultural policies, investment funds etc, especially as we already possess other requisites of a Common or Integrated Market which have yet to be achieved by the Six and can only be achieved with difficulty, viz., free movement of labour and capital etc.[15]

That would have been a curious twist indeed in the long tale of Irish nationalism, especially when so much of that tale had been concerned with 'the land question'. One of the deepest wells of support for Ireland's entry into the EC was the political wish to be recognised in nature rather than name as an independent country. For Ireland's Department of Agriculture to reason as it did is powerful evidence of how important the economic motivation for Irish membership was. When the Irish rural population was leaving the land at a rate roughly comparable with that in other west European countries after 1945, it was also leaving the country. At the time the Department of Agriculture made their comment, the population of Ireland was shrinking, even as elsewhere in western Europe population was rapidly rising with prosperity.

That Ireland shared with Poland in the nineteenth century a sacred place in the history of European nationalism as the two Catholic nations whose political substantiation the great powers forbade until shaken by war and revolution was of no political benefit in the materialistic mid-1950s. The OEEC secretariat officials saw the problem, as did Ireland's Department of Agriculture, as an economic one. Their assessment rested on rough and ready per capita income estimates, so that for them Ireland was a border-line case. In contrast, less-developed Portugal's case for entry into EFTA was thought stronger. EFTA was only about trade; the EEC was also about similarities in general economic policy. Thus, when it came to establishing the terms of Portugal's membership of EFTA, Portugal was treated very generously. It is unlikely that Ireland would have won comparable treatment. Without persistent protection, the Irish Department of Trade and Industry forecast, membership of EFTA would mean a loss of more than 50,000 Irish jobs through competition with British manufacturing and a further fall in population as emigrants left for Britain. At an OEEC Council Meeting in February 1957 the view of the Fianna Fáil government, which under Eamonn de Valera had just won the general election, was that the strict application of free trade principles was 'unthinkable', as these principles had 'left us terrible memories in Ireland'.[16] The government's ideas ran more along the lines of those of the Portuguese government, an initial ten-year period of membership without tariff reductions during which Ireland could still increase tariffs if necessary up to 50 per cent *ad valorem*. Only after ten years would they begin to be lowered, by 5 per cent a year. There were in fact in existing Irish tariff schedules about 150 tariffs as high as 50 per cent. There were also supplementary 'levies' in order to protect the balance of payments. No plea was made about the fate of Irish preferences in Britain.

To put these demands into perspective, before the French veto fell on the concept of a free trade area, Portugal seemed to have secured in negotiation a twelve-year initial transition period in which it would make only half the tariff reductions required of the other countries, rather less than what the Irish government hoped for. Nor had it secured the right to impose new tariffs in that period equal to the highest existing tariff applied by the other members. But it had secured a concession to impose new tariffs at the 'usual' rates used by Portugal. Whether these terms would have been finally offered to and accepted by Ireland we cannot be sure. Negotiations were broken off after the veto in November 1958.

That industry was the problem in widening Ireland's trading relationships had become clear to all in 1958. That the existing relationship with Britain, although resumed after the French veto, was now likely to be called into question again at any time was obvious. The goal of greater industrialisation, the objective for which so many high tariffs had been kept in place but with relatively poor results, became much more urgent, requiring more than tariff protection for its achievement. The sense within government was that there was not much time. And indeed there was not: in 1961 the United Kingdom applied for membership of the EEC.

The contrast between the Irish and Danish situations after the November 1958 veto of the free trade area is absolute and helps to explain their different experiences of industrialisation. What threatened Ireland, a British application to join the common market at a time which for Ireland was premature, was for Denmark a step, albeit one that was not to be finally taken, towards resolving a commercial dilemma. With the United Kingdom and Germany both inside the EEC the agricultural interest would be united behind Danish accession. Manufacturing would be less united, but it would have easier access to the great market of the EEC. Whereas in Ireland between 1958 and 1961 urgency meant that the domestic policy framework within which Irish manufacturing operated began to change drastically, in Denmark a similar urgency might only have emphasised the fractures within the Danish manufacturing interest which, as things stood, held its place in intra-Scandinavian trade and seemed confident of continuing to do so whatever the United Kingdom decided. The formation of EFTA in May 1960 only emphasised this difference. Denmark's two biggest industrial markets, Sweden and Norway, also became members of EFTA. Ireland did not, fear of losing some of its existing industry constituting an important motive.

With the formation of EFTA the same choices of policy faced Ireland as three years earlier. As with the earlier free trade area proposal, Britain sought to exclude agricultural trade from the agreement and Denmark demanded a price for entry and obtained it through a bilateral agreement with the United Kingdom reducing British tariffs on some Danish agricultural exports, guaranteeing that Danish producers of bacon would retain the same share of their British market under the new arrangements and would be given a share in any increase in imports. If quantitative import controls were imposed, Denmark would be given quotas which allowed it to retain its share of the market. Even before EFTA came into being, therefore, Ireland's alternative to membership of EFTA, some form of inclusion in an administrative rationalisation of the British food market, had been weakened. It emphasised Ireland's diplomatic weakness. Because the UK saw EFTA as a bargaining instrument against the common market it needed Denmark in EFTA. Its own market in Ireland was not threatened. Nor had Ireland anything to offer in terms of tariff reductions which would expand British markets there. That was confirmed, at least in British eyes, in Anglo–Irish talks from July 1959 onward.

In those talks the Irish edged closer to the Department of Agriculture's earlier idea that something resembling a common market in the agriculture of Ireland and Britain would be Ireland's best, or only feasible, way forward. It should create, the Department suggested, a closer relationship of agricultural prices between Britain and Ireland than existed inside the common market of the EEC. To a certain extent this had happened in the case of Irish cattle exported to Britain for fattening and slaughter. Irish farmers received prices that were related to, although not so high as, the price paid on slaughtering to the British farmer. The Irish government sought the extension of similar arrangements for other agricultural exports, leading to a co-ordinated development of agriculture in both countries with closely related price levels and so to an unrestricted access to the British market for Irish agricultural exports. In return there were concessions to be made to British manufactured exporters. Those fell well short of free trade. Nevertheless, the Irish government accepted that their impact would be to lower production in some Irish industries. The thrust of the proposal was thus to continue to ensure agricultural exports while introducing an element of competition into the domestic industrial scene. There was nothing in this to tempt the British government, nor, it seems, was there any point in making a better offer. Reginald Maudling, the British minister in charge of the negotiations, gave his plain opinion to the Irish taoiseach, Seán Lemass, that there was no trading concession Ireland could offer which would gain the agricultural arrangements that the Dublin government wanted.

Irish attention turned towards the EFTA negotiations and to the same point when in 1958 it had not pursued any further the possibility of membership of the European Free Trade Area; would it make sense to join EFTA if the same terms were available as those for which Portugal was negotiating? Those terms were that only Portuguese industries which exported would have to make the full tariff reductions of the other member states on the due dates. For other industries tariffs could be reduced at half the rate applying to other member states, so that in 1970 they would still be protected at half their level when the agreement had come into force. Further negotiations could then follow. The Irish Department of Industry and Commerce rejected this as too dangerous. Other ministries thought this might indeed be a way forward, the Department of Finance, provided that no better terms could be negotiated, and the Department of Foreign Affairs, for essentially political reasons, but they also thought that a free trade agreement with Britain alone might be a more advantageous choice. This was disputed by other government departments. It was in this sea of indecision that in spring 1961 evidence began to pile up that the United Kingdom was considering applying for membership of the European Communities. Ireland should, if that happened, Lemass stated in Dáil Éireann, itself consider membership or association if satisfactory terms could be obtained. The British decision to apply became public on the last day of July 1961 and on that same day Ireland applied for membership.

The discussions beforehand had all insisted on some recognition by the existing member-states of Ireland's economic development programmes, while most speakers in the Dáil stressed the fact that Irish membership must be dependent on that of the United Kingdom. Unlike Denmark, however, when it came to submitting the application Ireland did not specifically state it to be dependent on the success of the British application.

There were in the event almost no discussions with the European Commission on Ireland's 1961 application and certainly nothing that could reasonably be called a negotiation before, after fifteen months of negotiation with the United Kingdom, France in January 1963 vetoed United Kingdom membership. Afterwards President de Gaulle, in a personal meeting with the Danish Prime Minister Jens-Otto Krag, seemed to offer the possibility of membership to Denmark. Negotiations had gone further and faster with Denmark than with Ireland, after a very belated start, but it took the Danish Prime Minister only a night in a train to accept that, with Britain still in EFTA, accession to the EEC would not improve Denmark's position.

The possibility that the Common External Tariff of the EEC would separate Ireland from the United Kingdom market was the factor that had made for so few reservations about Ireland's decision to apply for Community membership. That in turn forced the pace of positive decisions about economic development. Industrialisation would have to take place with diminishing protection and so could not rely on tariffs as the sole incentive. With so small a domestic market, industrialisation had to be for export markets. Government financial assistance, the development of industrial training, tax favours, were all sketched out as a way to deal with the shock of adjustment to the common market. That the European Community was not expanded and eleven further years were to pass before either the United Kingdom or Ireland did join, did not alter the mood created out of the urgencies of 1958–61. The acceptance that industrialisation must go hand-in-hand with trade liberalisation became the core of national economic development planning. The role of the government was to provide impetus, financial backing and to make big changes in the fiscal system. It was well understood in Dublin through frequent talks with the British government that, for all its flirtations with the Commonwealth in the early years of the decade, British foreign policy was set on EEC membership if and when it should prove possible. In mid-February 1965 Prime Minister Harold Wilson made the position public in the House of Commons. After increasing their majority in the general election of March 1966 his government decided in late October that it would again seek admission. It did so in May 1967, only to encounter another French veto. The application, however, was not withdrawn.

By then, rethinking industrialisation policy for a less protected environment had brought a change in Ireland's trading relations with Britain. The Anglo-Irish Free Trade Agreement, negotiated through 1965 and signed in December of that year, meant the rapid removal of most British tariffs on Irish manufactured goods and a more delayed removal of Irish tariffs on British manufactures. It was not universally popular in the Dáil, for it could be presented as acceptance of British commercial domination, but it was about far more than increasing trade to and from the United Kingdom. Unlike the Irish attempts at bilateral trade agreements with Britain in the late 1950s, it catered for the growth of manufactured exports and, most importantly, it looked towards the entry of both countries into the common market.[17] Lemass considered the agreement as a possible base for temporarily entering EFTA as a step towards the desired goal of the EEC, but that required an EEC–EFTA agreement which was not in sight.

The Anglo-Irish Free Trade Agreement's effect is partly captured in Table 2.5 by the steep fall of agricultural products in the value of total Irish exports between 1965 and 1970, both to the United Kingdom and to the world. The proportion of all Irish exports going to Britain continued after 1965 to shrink at more or less the same rate that it was shrinking before. In the case of agricultural exports, however, the Agreement did initially increase the share directed to the British market. With entry of both countries into the EEC, the picture began to change and agriculture as well as industry did increasingly find markets on the continent.

The fact that it was the British decision to try to join the common market which determined the Irish and Danish decisions to do the same should not lead to any overestimation of the similarity of the two countries' positions or intentions. Agricultural exports were very important to the decision. They were competitors in the British market for agricultural produce and would remain so under more guaranteed conditions and receiving higher prices under the regime of the Common Agricultural Policy. As manufacturing trade grew in relative importance for both, however, the divergence of their political and economic behaviour in the common market and the European Community became more apparent.

Although accession to the EU cancelled the privileged position of Dutch agricultural exports over Danish to Germany, two salient facts prevailed. The institutional structures stretching from Danish pig and dairy farmers to food distributors and retailers in the United Kingdom continued to give Denmark an advantage in a market where its food exports had been so long and well established. Second, the income elasticity of demand for food grew so feebly in the 1970s in both Britain and Germany that gaining a stronger position on the now more easily accessible German market was not quite the alluring prospect that it had seemed in the 1950s. The United Kingdom retained its primary importance as an outlet for Danish agricultural exports. Germany's manufacturing imports continued to grow at a high rate, offering Denmark much better prospects than the struggle for advantage on a relatively static agricultural market. Yet Danish trade in manufactures in these propitious circumstances did not shift towards the German market significantly. Scandinavia, at first Norway and Sweden, later with the addition of Finland, remained the main market.

Writing in 1993, the Danish political scientist and historian, Vibeke Sørensen, offered an explanation for this exceptional pattern of distribution of Danish foreign trade. In the 1950s, she argued, Danish governments, while seeking industrialisation, were concerned to protect the industrial sectors which they wished to develop. In their eyes this meant primarily protection against German exports. In part this was because protection against German manufactured exports was thought by trade unions to protect Danish industrial jobs and persistence with a policy of high employment levels. The trade union vote was important to the Danish Social Democrats. She traced this concern with industrial protection to Denmark's comparatively mild experience of the inter-war Great Depression and the political stability which the country enjoyed when much of Europe was in political turmoil. That stability was based on a political consensus of which one element was a measure of insulation from the international economy. To this was added in the 1950s the need to manage the balance of payments very carefully. The growing welfare state required adjusting industry to international markets without increasing unemployment. Industrialisation therefore was understood as having crucial domestic objectives which should not be endangered.[18] In these circumstances, Sørensen argued, government, industry and trade unions colluded to restrict the volume of trade with the German Federal Republic, a practice which persisted for similar reasons after accession to the European Community. As she wrote, Denmark 'demonstrated a remarkable will to shape its own national destiny in the post-war period'.[19]

That last remark is equally valid for Ireland. They both refuted the theoretical assumption that small states cannot impose their own strategies. In Denmark's case indeed, Sørensen argues that an international politico-economic strategy governed the role of the manufacturing sector through the inter-war period and beyond the 1960s. Industrial protection was ended by entry into the common market, but the idea of protection was transmuted into the will to find an international marketing framework in which Denmark could industrialise through exports, but do so safely. Safely meant limiting the interchange with the German Federal Republic when that very interchange was the most potent stimulus to the growth of the manufacturing sector across almost the whole of western Europe.

Fears that the developing industrial interchanges with Germany would make the adjustment of Danish manufacturing to the impending trade liberalisation in western Europe more difficult were one cause of the persistent efforts to create some form of Nordic customs union.[20] Social Democrats wanted a customs union which would enlarge the marketing possibilities for Danish manufactures, allowing larger scale production by Danish industry and so preserving employment by internationalising Denmark's industry while sheltering it from German competition. This was entirely a concept for the industrial sector, for Norway and Sweden would, it was assumed, maintain their high levels of agricultural protection. Manufactures made up 44 per cent of intra-Nordic trade in the 1950s. There were Danish hopes that in some way the project as it existed at the time of the free trade area negotiations might be linked with a change of heart by the United Kingdom to open the free trade area to agricultural exports, but these hopes were vain. When a Danish government inquiry suggested in 1958 that the opening of all OEEC markets by a free trade agreement with the EEC would mean export gains by Denmark which would surpass in value any losses from increased competition, reactions in Danish industry remained in favour of protection, preferably within a Nordic customs union, behind a common 'Nordic' tariff. Exports of machinery were for Denmark, Norway and Sweden greater inside the potential Nordic union than to Germany.

What came instead were the Common External Tariff of the EEC and Danish membership of EFTA, followed by the 1961 British decision to apply for membership of EEC. By the British decision all Danish agricultural interests, from large-scale farmers whose sales were in Germany to smallholders who produced much of the butter and bacon that went to Britain, were reconciled. A Danish application would become politically practicable if manufacturing interests and workers could be brought to change their position. When the Danish application was made it included reservations on the free movement of persons and of labour and also a reservation on social policy. There being no agreement between the six EEC member-states on these issues as yet, those reservations were no immediate impediment to membership. The French veto on British entry, however, left Danish agriculture to concentrate energetically on its British market, while Danish manufacturing still stood ready to give support to any Scandinavian customs union which would encourage the further growth of its intra-Scandinavian trade in manufactures.

When de Gaulle resigned as President of France on 28 April 1969 such a scheme was in the course of being discussed at the highest level under the name of 'Nordek'. It may be wondered why the Nordic project still attracted such interest when Denmark, Norway and Sweden were all EFTA members and Finland had a special trade agreement with EFTA. The answer has to be in part a political one, the attraction of a project which linked the Danish Social Democrats to the Social Democratic Parties of Norway and Sweden, both of which exercised more power in their respective countries than their Danish counterpart. For the Social Democrats the hope prevailed that an economic model which did more to preserve employment, which offered more, and more secure, welfare and avoided deflationary adjustment to the international economy, high interest rates and pressures to keep down wages, might become a common Scandinavian policy.[21] The German Federal Republic seemed in this light to represent an antithetical model. It was easy to draw the conclusion, no matter how prejudiced or over-optimistic, that the embrace of Nordek would offer a better future to Danish industry than would that of Germany, that the Scandinavian welfare state was in some way morally and ethically superior to the German model, and that increased trade in manufactures with Germany foreshadowed not only higher levels of unemployment but lower levels of social, and therefore national, coherence. The nature of the appeal was emotional and aspirational; the reasoning behind it lacked that very coherence with which it was intended to endow Scandinavia.

It was the meeting at The Hague of the leaders of the six EEC states in December 1969 which, by deciding to open negotiations with the four applicant states, relegated Nordek to a lower priority for Denmark. A Nordic economic and social union became subsidiary to negotiating entry into EEC, because of the attraction of the common market to farmers rather than to Danish manufacturing. The Social Democrats had performed poorly in the 1968 general election. The centre-right parties, Venstre and the Conservatives, now insisted that Nordek should not be an objective on its own but rather a step towards Community membership.[22] When the text of the Nordek treaty was completed in February 1972 the Danes stipulated that any changes in Danish tariffs consequent on the treaty, but which were also of importance in negotiations with the Community, should not come into operation until 1 January 1974, one year after they hoped to enter the common market. Furthermore, the text of the Nordek treaty included a clause allowing the possibility of withdrawing from its terms at one year's notice, copying EFTA's example.

Divisions of interest between agriculture and industry, aspirations towards a common Scandinavian position, anxieties about future economic and political relationships with Germany, might all have had diminishing importance when the gates to the common market began to open had it not been for the domestic constitutional hurdles on the way to membership. The previous chapter emphasised the extent to which negotiating membership of the Community and then negotiating its national acceptance were political processes of such importance for the future that economic interest, even where economic gains seemed highly probable, was relegated everywhere to a subordinate role in the political process of discussion of the future of the nation. In that discussion the meaning of 'the nation' became whatever any group or individual wanted it to be or imagined it to have been. Vague sentiment, unachievable aspirations, myths and hard economic and political realities competed on equal ground. This was true of all applicant states, but nowhere were the constitutional arrangements so designed to produce competition and division as in Denmark.

The Danish constitution of 1953 specifically allowed surrenders of sovereignty to a supranational institution, but only to a clearly defined extent and only under political conditions that were very hard to meet. There were two possible procedures. The shorter one required approval by a majority of five-sixths of the members of the Folketing. There was another longer procedure demanded by the opponents of Danish accession at the time of Denmark's first application in 1961 when there was a five-sixths majority in the Folketing in favour of entry, involving a change in the constitution. To change the constitution required at first only a simple majority in favour of such a step in the Folketing. But the parliamentary vote had to be followed by a general election, after which the Folketing must again demonstrate by vote that there was still a desire for the change. If there was, there then had to be a referendum in which at least 40 per cent of the eligible voters must vote in favour of the new constitution. De Gaulle's veto on British membership meant that neither procedure had to be attempted. Either procedure constituted a political screening by which even the most coherent of political parties could be reduced to fragments. After the 1968 election eight parties were represented in the Folketing: the Social Democratic Party, the Justice Party, the Christian People's Party, the Conservative Party, Venstre and the Social Liberals. The Social Democrats, the biggest party since 1932, had recorded their lowest share of the vote since 1945 and the stability which they had previously brought to coalitions had given way to increasing governmental fragmentation, making the constitutional obstacles to accession yet more dangerous.

The hope of the government after the summit in The Hague in December 1969 was to adopt as pro-Community a stance and to negotiate for as small a list of requests as possible. One reason for this negotiating policy was that it seemed a tactic suitable to a situation where the support of five-sixths of the parliament might be needed. However, if we take as they arose the issues over which Denmark did wish to negotiate concessions, we can see how those issues evolved from points which at first did not seem divisive into issues of fundamental controversy.

The parliamentary motion passed on 11 May 1967 in favour of a second Danish application to the Community at the same time as the second British application, had not only made it clear that Danish membership and British membership hung together but had been equally explicit that the Danish application was in the expectation that the other Scandinavian countries would reach satisfactory relationships with an enlarged EEC. Norway applied for membership. Sweden, as a neutral country, could only explore a relationship short of full membership. It was unwilling to compromise its internationally recognised neutrality and the EC, in its turn, was unwilling to face the question of whether it should accept a neutral as a member-state. The possibility after the summit in The Hague that Denmark would withdraw from Nordek and that this might be the definitive collapse of the long-sustained hopes for a pan-Scandinavian trading area, did more to promote divisions inside the Conservative and the Social Democratic Parties than to heal them. The application itself opened a rift on a different issue within Venstre, some of whose parliamentary representatives, perhaps even a majority of them, would have been content with Danish membership in the EC even without the United Kingdom becoming a member. The text of the Nordek treaty was read in the light of what it might mean for Scandinavia's future as much as Denmark's.

These divisions became less important when Finland was forced by Soviet pressure to reject the terms of the Nordek treaty on 24 March 1970 and the treaty text therefore could not come into force. But if the elimination of the Scandinavian solution, without it being any fault of Denmark's, reunified one party, Venstre, it caused other problems for the Conservatives, some of whose Folketing representatives, including the Minister of Justice, were now unhappier in joining the Community with the easily envisageable further damage to the Scandinavian solution if no satisfactory links between Sweden and the Community would be formed. Nor were all liberals of one mind. The Radical Liberals had favoured the Nordek Treaty, of which Venstre was somewhat suspicious, as a guarantee that the Danish welfare state would not be eroded by the European Community. This position had allowed them to support Venstre's policy to join the Community. Without Sweden things looked less reassuring. At the parliamentary level they remained in favour of EEC membership, but one of their number, Poul Overgaard Nielsen became one of the leaders of the People's Movement Against the European

Community. Outside the Folketing they were moving into outright opposition.

They were by no means without sympathisers in the Social Democratic Party. The Social Democratic leader, Jens-Otto Krag, had installed Ivar Nørgaard, the editor of his party's newspaper, as Minister of Foreign Economic Affairs and Nordic Relations, in the 'Market Committee' whose task was to define the negotiating tactics for accession, perhaps in order to strengthen party unity and in doing so to shackle Nørgaard's reservations about the Community. It was a central aspect of Danish tactics for accession to emphasise Denmark's *communautaire* spirit. In his later career Nørgaard was to oppose the Single European Act and the Economic and Monetary Union.[23] At the start of June 1970 two Conservative ministers insisted that some form of formal Nordic cooperation be maintained after accession. How much stronger might various dissensions have been had it not still been the opinion that Norway would become a member of the Community at the same time as Denmark?

The importance of the political symbolism of a Scandinavian ideal was not confined to the Social Democratic movement, even if it was that movement which chiefly had driven forward the idea of a Scandinavian common market. The seeming loss of all hopes of a common Nordic solution stimulated fears in Danish parties that the EC member-states had political systems which were inadequately democratic and fed the thought that entry into the European Community might lead to a deterioration in the quality of Denmark's democracy. Two issues were particularly prone to enhance that sentiment. Did the European Community's wish to establish an institutional form of foreign policy co-ordination, European Political Cooperation, mean a loss of independent national political decision-making about security? For a country where sentiments in favour of neutrality were far from dead, this was a question which led to dangerous waters. Second, would the monetary union envisaged in ten years' time by the Werner Plan mean a further loss of sovereignty inside the Community through the loss of fiscal independence and of the ability of Denmark to conduct its own monetary policy?

The general assurances of government, that the European Commission's ambitions to unify Europe politically had been shattered by de Gaulle's 'vacant chair' policy in 1966–7 and that the idea of majority voting in Brussels overriding issues of fundamental importance to the smaller states had been permanently killed by the 'Luxembourg Compromise' of 1967 which resolved the crisis, had a hollow ring when the Gaullist, Raymond Barre, was pushing proposals in Brussels for some common monetary system, even if this fell well short of a plan for monetary union. A permanent institution for European Political Cooperation was not what the government had advertised to the electorate. The issues, it seemed, no longer just related to farmers' incomes, bacon, butter and eggs, but to how much sovereignty, if any, would be left to little Denmark, bound by treaty to the country which had occupied it thirty years earlier, and within a dubiously democratic, supranational form of governance on which it might exercise little influence. And at the end of the negotiating process lay the need either for five-sixths of the Folketing to vote for the treaty or, the path which Krag eventually chose, an election followed by a referendum.

Denmark, not wishing to discuss issues of security in the proposed European Political Cooperation forum, proposed discussing them there only on condition that NATO remained the central forum for all decisions about defence and security policy. A common monetary system was supported by the two centre-right parties, but the Radical Liberals veered between scepticism and hostility to the same plan. Their impact on the left wing of the Social Democrats on the monetary proposal was strong. Some Social Democrats were openly critical in parliament of the idea of eventual monetary union. Krag had reason to meditate on how substantial a group of Social Democrats had opposed the first application in 1961 as well as the present application when first made in 1967.

By the late autumn of 1970, as the negotiations proceeded, the Social Democrats in effect had added to the two earlier conditions for accession, British membership and satisfactory arrangements for other Scandinavian countries, two further conditions. There was to be no surrender of control over national economic, social and fiscal policy within a European monetary union and no discussion of defence and security policy within the European Political Cooperation framework, where political cooperation was not to develop in a supranational direction. In effect, therefore, they were almost confining their support for Danish accession to an entirely economic set of arrangements. Krag himself was attracted by the idea of European political union, although it appears as though his assurances about the effect of the Luxembourg Compromise were honestly delivered. Practical politician as he was, he thought the 'Compromise' was also an accurate estimate of how far Denmark could be led.

This did not still the rising tide of suspicion about life within the EC. Another issue arose to lessen still further Denmark's hopes of an unperturbed negotiation. Did the 'right to establishment' proclaimed by the Rome Treaty imply the right of foreigners – Germans were meant – to buy second homes on the Danish seacoast? The Danish laws which governed the purchase of property by foreigners for non-commercial reasons normally required a permit from the Ministry of Justice. Conservationists and xenophobes met in what might have proved a common cause but failed to become so. The issue was still not settled by September 1971 when the centre-right parties lost a general election to the Social Democrats and

Krag returned as Prime Minister to achieve the accession of which he had been thwarted in 1963.

By a manoeuvre whose constitutional correctness was questionable he had earlier persuaded his party, perhaps out of fear of losing another election, to call for a referendum, not on the constitutionally necessary grounds that accession to the Community was a constitutional change, but on the more general grounds that a decision to join should in any case be ratified by the population as a whole. In trying to remove EEC membership from a central position in the electoral campaign by promising a referendum if he was victorious he seemed by an elliptical route to be institutionalising a new concept that a referendum was the *only* means by which Danish sovereignty could be surrendered. It looked easier by that route than by winning five-sixths of a Folketing vote.

The referendum campaign, in spite of the fact that for most of its duration the opinion polls reported that there would be a comfortable majority for accession, inevitably exacerbated still further the political division within, as well as between, parties over what had become central issues. The government relied heavily on economic arguments for accession, claiming that a failure to join the EC would mean that the value of agricultural exports would remain about 30 per cent lower than would be the case if Denmark joined the common market. It argued that, far from the welfare state being in danger, it would be preserved only through EC membership; failure to join would mean that it was the poorest in Denmark who would suffer most. The Danish krone, Krag insisted, would have to be devalued if Denmark stayed outside the Community. The one moment of real anxiety that opinion polls gave to the government was when Norway independently decided on its own date for the national referendum on entry to which it was committed.

The debate within Norway had done nothing to encourage hopes of Scandinavian unity. Opinion polls throughout the campaign indicated a majority against accession, although neither side in the campaign appears to have believed that that would be the outcome. Denmark received little or no attention, except perhaps that its poll results encouraged the Norwegian Social Democrats to deceive themselves. Trygve Bratteli, the Norwegian Labour Party Prime Minister, did not want to collude with Denmark to determine the referendum dates. He hoped, nevertheless, that Denmark would choose an earlier date than Norway, perhaps in June 1972, and that the result would sway Norwegian opinion in favour of joining. Krag, seemingly by himself and without consultation, opted for a later date.[24] In the aftermath of the rejection of membership by the Norwegian electorate the Danish opinion polls wobbled. The referendum date, 25 September 1972, was then used by Norwegian enthusiasts for Nordek to proclaim that day 'a chance for the Nordic countries'.[25] The Danish referendum, however, confirmed what the opinion polls had so consistently predicted. In retrospect it can be seen that the idea of Scandinavia and a Scandinavian solution divided the Norwegian Labour Party as much as the Danish Social Democrats and that, as in Denmark, all parties were divided deeply by the referendum campaign.[26]

In spite of the result, the national debate and the referendum campaign in Denmark transformed what had looked at first like a straightforward economic choice into a victory over a suspiciously uneasy, voluble and numerous minority whose objections to Community membership were based on points of political principle. In indicating to the European Commission its assent to the terms of membership the government felt obliged to state that it was not in favour of the European Political Cooperation forum having any control over security policy, which properly belonged to NATO, and that it would not be, as things presently stood, in favour of economic and monetary union. These statements were registered from the chair of the meeting with the European Commission by Aldo Moro, the Italian Prime Minister, as statements of current opinion about proposals on which decisions lay only in the future. It was sensible on his part to treat them as positions which might change over time. In 1992, however, in another referendum Danish voters rejected the terms of the Treaty of Maastricht and Denmark did not join the European Economic and Monetary Union. The referendum campaign of 1972 had opened the road to Denmark's position as a member-state where opinion polls repeatedly showed low levels of support for the European Union.

This account of the political background to Denmark's accession is not primarily intended, however, to explain Denmark's subsequent political attitudes to the EC/EU. It is intended to illustrate the political background to Danish commercial policy within the EC/EU and to point out the contrast with Ireland's more confident response to Community membership. The difference between Irish and Danish parliamentary and public opinion was greatly widened by the processes of negotiation with the Six and of national referendums.

In Ireland, by contrast, the processes of negotiation and referendum appeared more as a confirmation of sovereignty than a surrender of it. The 'yes' vote in the referendum was 83 per cent of the total vote. The two major parliamentary parties, Fianna Fáil and Fine Gael, both campaigned for a 'yes' vote, leaving only the smaller Labour Party to campaign unconvincingly against entry. The peacefulness of the campaign and the massive majority, and the contrast with Denmark, in themselves concentrate our attention more on the political differences between the two countries than their similarity as agricultural exporters with smaller scale industrial sectors. Widespread though ignorance of the political structure of the Community and indifference to its political purposes were in Ireland, there was no enmity and little suspicion towards it. It was optimistically viewed as a political framework in which Ireland could play a more cosmopolitan role than in its narrow relationship with the United Kingdom.

Economic gain was not, in any case for any of the applicants, separate from the concept of political gain. The idea that economic gain will strengthen a country's bargaining position in world politics unavoidably raises the question, for what exact political purpose an increase in economic strength is needed. Since that increased power must logically in part be deployed within the supranational organisation, the second question immediately arises for what the supranational organisation itself should stand. Denmark's accession was on a programme, which received more support after accession, of restricting the scope of the organisation. Ireland had hopes that it would gain by allowing the organisation a fuller scope. Many Danes evidently thought of the EC as a challenge to the political and economic comforts which Denmark enjoyed. The government appeal for a 'yes' vote was not 'enrichissez-vous!'. It was rather an appeal for support for a step which would sustain Denmark's economic security and prevent disturbance to its socio-economic balance. The analogy is more with the argument at the same time of the British government that EEC membership would restore prosperity to British manufacturing and reverse the changes in that sector erroneously referred to as 'decline'. Preserving British industry with the help of 'Europe' would, it was thought, restore some of Britain's lost international political influence while sustaining employment in manufacturing. If there could be a reactionary element in Britain's application, there could be a cautiously conservative element in Denmark's. In Norway the campaign to persuade voters to reject accession to the EC drew increasingly on 'traditional' aspects of Norwegian life seen as menaced by European integration. In Denmark the groups campaigning for a 'no' vote forecast the end of the welfare state, the loss of political independence, the eventual destruction of any common political concept of Scandinavia and sharp falls in industrial income. It was difficult to campaign in favour of the economic past in Ireland.

A follow-up survey after the Danish referendum, aimed at finding out more exactly the population's motives for voting as it had done, implied that a substantial proportion of those approving membership would have preferred some form of looser 'association' because it would have been safer, less committing.[27] To what extent this was a long-held view or to what extent it was a reaction to the exaggerated claims made by both sides in the referendum campaign itself were not objects of the inquiry. For a historian the method of asking people to compare on the one hand a decision which they had made about an actual problem to a decision about a hypothetical problem which they had not been required to make generates dubious evidence. 'Association' was not on offer. The more precise historical question was to ask whether the referendum campaign had not made voters wish that there was a third choice. Petersen's analyses of the referendum do, nonetheless, suggest, although not prove, that the yearning for an alternative arrangement survived and may even have been stimulated by the referendum campaign, although Nordek by then was dead.

Petersen's analyses also show that half of the voters surveyed justified their referendum vote with economic reasons. Only 15.5 per cent did so with political reasons. These figures were probably not influenced by the nature of the referendum campaign. With both sides in the campaign threatening economic hardship, voters were faced with what was presented as an immediate economic choice of which the adverse political effects, if such there were, were a more distant problem. This perspective was not false. There was an economic choice to be registered and the evidence is strong that a clear majority of the country was in favour of entry. Political objections to membership of the European Community may in those circumstances have been held by many who voted for entry. Among those objections would have been reluctance to abandon the idea of a Scandinavian economic and political association, fears that industries might suffer from competition from Germany inside the EEC, anxieties that Germany, where the Netherlands competed on equal terms, might prove a harder agricultural market to sell on than Britain and beliefs, or prejudices, that political systems inside the European Community fell well short of Danish standards. Contrast these anxieties with Ireland's certainty to win a new market for agricultural exports at better prices than its main existing market and to win a new market for manufactured exports. Furthermore, Ireland was able to negotiate acceptance by the Six that its national development plans, by which was mostly meant its industrialisation programmes, would be accepted in principle as not being unfair competition. Ireland was certain to make substantial financial gains from the Common Agricultural Policy and through devaluing the Irish 'green' pound it was able to make them yet more substantial. It might seem paradoxical that so recently independent a country should have been so politically optimistic over a surrender of some of the sovereignty that it had fought so hard for, but accession and the larger market acknowledged the fact that it was indeed independent.

It would be incorrect to attribute the rapid growth of Ireland's manufactured exports entirely to accession to the Community, for it was in the decade before entry that some of the significant changes took place and can be measured. Nevertheless, the first twenty years inside the EEC/EU transformed the Irish economy through a growth of industrial output and exports akin to some of the spectacular bursts of industrialisation experienced by other western European economies in the nineteenth century.

The most authoritative studies of Irish industrialisation after entry into the Community present a gloomy picture of the impact of accession on what Irish writers like to call 'indigenous' industry, Irish-owned manufacturing which preceded the new foreign-owned industries which came after entry into the common market. Particular acts of industrial policy are singled out in most accounts as being of particular importance in the Irish experience of industrialisation after accession, especially those which attracted 'non-indigenous' industry. In most European countries for which we have long-run studies of industrialisation, it is usually shown to have depended on complex international, domestic and regional interactions. In Ireland the industrialisation boom which followed entry into the EC was driven by the exceptionally favourable terms given to direct foreign investment in manufacturing. Where state priming of industrialisation, through tariff policy, fiscal policy, state purchasing of military goods, or simple subsidy, privileged monopoly or oligopoly rights, was pursued in the past, it frequently made little or even no lasting contribution to building a successful industrial sector. It achieved somewhat more where governments were despotisms, although what they created was of uncertain durability. Ireland does not qualify as a despotism. Yet particular acts of Irish government policy do serve as markers in the timing of rapid industrialisation and they were specifically intended to take advantage of common market membership.

The two aspects of Irish industrialisation policy which receive the most attention are the successful negotiation with the EEC before entry to have the country's status as a less developed economy recognised by the EEC's agreement to accept in principle the Irish government's financial support for industrial development rather than automatically condemning it as state aid in breach of the Community's competition policy. This was achieved by leaving the request until almost the end of the negotiation, in mid-October 1971. The Irish argument was made in the context of regional inequalities, an issue about which the European Commission had become worried. Irish diplomats argued that one purpose of their industrial development policy was to reduce such inequalities. The argument was accepted by the Commission in this context in a statement made from the chair by Aldo Moro, his speech indicating also the Commission's intention to introduce its own regional policy. When that policy was eventually formulated, the whole of Ireland was deemed to be a 'region' for the purposes of development aid.

One aspect of Irish policy did fall foul eventually of the European Commission: company and corporation tax pardons for foreign direct investment, creating what were in effect tax-free enclaves for foreign firms. The success of this policy in attracting foreign investment was remarkable. Irish wages were lower at first than in any other member-state and that, combined with the tax holiday, attracted foreign capital, especially from the

USA, looking for a production base inside the Community tariff. Between 1973 and 1983 employment in 'indigenous' industry fell by 17,000; in 'foreign' industry it rose by 25,000.[28] The gross output of foreign new industry rose between 1973 and 1985 by about £520 million in constant prices; that of the rest of Irish industry by £206 million.[29] In that manufacturing sector where change was most rapid, engineering, in Irish-owned firms the biggest share of employment between 1973 and 1987 was always in firms of fifty or fewer workers. In foreign-owned firms it was always in firms with more than 200 employees.[30]

Foreign firms settling in Ireland were entitled to grants on the same terms as new Irish firms. Their main purpose in settling there was to export, so that their impact on the balance of payments was beneficial. As EC Competition Policy evolved it was difficult to sustain for long the argument that the tax exemption was not discriminatory inside a common market and the European Commission eventually ruled it to be so. Ireland's response was to forego yet more realisable tax income by imposing a flat 10 per cent rate for all corporation tax, whether on foreign or native firms, by the measure of the other EU states a very low rate. It is probably impossible to estimate accurately the export share of 'non-indigenous' industry, but the pattern of growth and the commodity structure of Irish exports are evidence suggestive of its importance.

Irish agriculture made a substantially greater contribution in 1945 to national product, about 37 per cent of the total, than manufacturing and construction, accountable for about 17 per cent. It was between 1955 and 1960, with the first steps towards lowering industrial protection and a more purposive effort to diversify Ireland's manufacturing exports that manufacturing and construction overtook agriculture's share of national product. By 1970 agriculture's share had fallen to 14 per cent, still high by western European standards. A closer and more accurate picture of the growth in manufacturing industry is provided by the growth in the volume of industrial output. This grew between 1951 and 1958 at an average of 1.3 per cent per year, between 1958 and 1973 at 6.7 per cent. After a slowdown over 1973–6 to 1.2 per cent, it then grew over the period 1976–9 by an average of 9.1 per cent annually. It slowed again to grow at only 1.5 per cent in 1979–82 and afterwards over the period 1982–7 it grew by 6.3 per cent annually.[31]

The picture is one of three dynamic industrialisation booms; one whose beginning coincided with the shock of the free trade area negotiations, the second with adjustment to membership of the EC interrupted by the cyclical downturn of 1979, and a third in the 1980s. Each one was associated with a remarkably vigorous growth of exports and with rapid change in the composition of total output and total exports. The figures confirm the historical narrative that trade liberalisation in Europe, specifically the formation of the European Economic Community and the United Kingdom's response to it, imparted a shock to Ireland's political economy and initiated a roller-coaster journey to economic development whose later most dynamic phases depended on joining the EEC. It was crucial that from the date of Ireland's accession the EEC also included the United Kingdom, Ireland's biggest market. The continuing importance of the UK market has been analysed by O'Donnell.[32] Tables 2.6–2.8 include O'Donnell's conclusions in a more complicated setting by indicating the importance of the UK market in the two booms after accession to the EC and also by including the annual growth rates of trade values, partly to give a clearer picture of the United Kingdom's role in Ireland's industrial growth and partly to emphasise the volatility of Ireland's manufacturing exports.

It can be seen in Table 2.6 that accession produced a high growth rate of exports to the EC. Their rate of growth to the British market was nevertheless

Table 2.6 Two Irish trade booms – A

	1974	1975	1976	1977	1978	1979	1980
Growth of total exports (current values) %	34.4	12.3	1.3	27.8	38.2	19.9	21.2
Growth of exports to EC-9 (current values) %	21.6	28.2	Negative	33.5	31.3	32.4	18.1
Growth of exports to UK as % of growth of exports to EC-9 (current values) %	42.6	61.2	Negative	48.0	37.1	54.2	19.6
% growth rate of real GDP per capita							
Ireland	4.3	2.0	2.2	6.8	5.8	3.4	3.7
EC	1.6	–1.2	5.1	2.4	3.3	3.4	0.0

Table 2.7 Two Irish trade booms – B

	1986	1987	1988	1989	1990
Growth of total exports (current values) %	22.4	27.5	18.3	9.0	17.4
Growth of exports to EC-12 (current values) %	24.8	30.6	18.4	6.7	18.6
Growth of exports to UK as % of growth of exports to EC-12 (current values) %	51.0	42.7	48.9	79.6	61.8
% growth rate of real GDP per capita					
Ireland	3.1	4.7	5.2	5.8	8.5
EC	2.8	2.9	4.3	3.5	2.5

Table 2.8 Two Irish trade booms. Most significant increases in commodity export groups (SITC-2 digit)

A. 1973–80

Live animals, meat and meat preparations, miscellaneous food preparations; organic and inorganic chemicals; chemical materials and products; machinery (non-electric)

B. 1985–90

Miscellaneous edible products and preparations; medical and pharmaceutical products; paper, paperboard, and articles of pulp, paper and paperboard; power-generating machinery and equipment; miscellaneous manufactured articles

---

much higher than to the rest of the EC. This was probably accentuated by a lower growth rate of GDP in 1974 in the original six states of the European Community and a negative one in 1975. Irish exports shrank in current values to both the EC and the UK in 1976 in spite of the economic upturn. The next four years, 1977–80, were characterised by very high rates of GDP growth in Ireland and very large increases in exports to the EC. The UK market now was responsible for rather less than half of the increase in exports. The slowing-down in 1980 reflected the stagnation of the European Community's economies in that year, although Ireland's economy still grew vigorously until the hard times of 1981. The second half of the 1980s however was to witness another boom in Irish exports to the EC leading to even higher domestic growth rates than in the 1970s and in every year higher, sometimes much higher, than in the rest of the European Community.

   Looking at the differences in the commodity structure of Irish exports over the course of these two spectacular export booms it can be seen (Table 2.8) that in the first of them primary agricultural exports played their part, whereas in the second boom the big increases in food exports were in processed or manufactured food preparations. Otherwise, in the second boom the biggest increases were in manufactured exports, especially from the complex of paper industries, from pharmaceutical producers and from electrical engineering.

   A striking aspect of the 1986–90 boom is that the growth in the value of exports to the United Kingdom was in every year by far the greatest contribution to the growth of total exports to the European Community, in the last two years 1989–90 remarkably so (Table 2.7). To return to the observation at the outset that Denmark and Ireland were exceptional in so far as it was not with Germany that their exports and imports of manufactures grew most rapidly, there would seem to be for Ireland an explanation in that once both Ireland and the UK were within the Common External Tariff of the

Community Ireland provided a cheaper base for 'foreign' firms manufacturing for the British market, as it had done to some extent earlier in a less dynamic context for British firms.

In 1960, the share of agricultural exports (SITC 0) in total Danish and Irish exports was almost the same, in both cases more than a half. Between 1960 and 1970 it fell much more rapidly for Denmark than for Ireland (Table 2.9). From the date of entry into the EC the share of agricultural products in Denmark's total exports began to decline much more slowly. In Ireland's total exports the strong trend towards a growing share of manufactured exports was uninterrupted, so that by 1988, on the eve of the Single European Act, it was greater than that for Danish exports.

It cannot be argued that Ireland's concentration on the British market and the relatively limited value of its trade in manufactures with Germany slowed down either its industrialisation or its growth. Its choice for the European Community worked strongly in favour of both. The ten years between 1963 and 1973 when it could not join were years of powerful export growth and industrial development because the Anglo-Irish Free Trade Agreement of December 1965 linked Irish domestic industrial policy to the outside world in so far as it was consciously perceived as a step beyond Britain towards the European Community, and that further step was seen as part of a programme of national revival. The economic arguments carried Ireland down this adventurous path, but they were also in themselves the political motive for joining. As a later taoiseach, Garett Fitzgerald, was to point out in a lecture, Ireland had been neutral in the Second World War, was not a member of NATO, was not particularly motivated to use economic integration to make war impossible between western European countries, had few strategic concerns in Europe and had little interest in the development of a European identity.[33] He could have added that it became the only member-state of the European Community which claimed, incorrectly, in its constitution to be ruling a substantial part of another member-state. Its real politics had to be in shaping its economic future.

Table 2.9 Agricultural exports (SITC 0) as a percentage of total exports of Denmark and Ireland, 1960–88

	Denmark (%)	Ireland (%)
1960	54.80	54.09
1970	33.83	45.48
1980	30.74	34.34
1988	26.59	23.57

Source: OECD, Department of Economics and Statistics, *Foreign Trade by Commodities*, annual volumes.

How successful, in comparison, was Denmark's choice? Throughout the 1960s the share of Danish exports going to the common market had shown a stable falling trend. One factor in the higher growth rate of exports to the rest of the world than to the common market in the 1960s was that EFTA facilitated exports to Norway and Sweden. The share of exports going to those two countries in the period 1961–3 to 1970–2 rose by almost as much as the share going to the nine-member European Economic Community fell. While accession to the common market had the effect of reducing the share of exports to Norway and Sweden, it did not do so by much, leaving that share still at the level of 1967. Accession to the European Community thus initially established Denmark's export trade balanced on a tripod of markets, Scandinavia, Germany and the United Kingdom. After 1975 Germany replaced the United Kingdom as Denmark's single biggest national market and over the period 1976–90 exports to Germany grew by 373 per cent in current prices and to the United Kingdom by only 186 per cent.

This might imply that EC membership achieved its aims by enabling Denmark to substitute the most rapidly growing and the biggest market for semi-manufactures and engineering products, Germany, for what had been primarily a market for foodstuffs, the United Kingdom, while at the same time securing a bigger market for agricultural exports in Germany than it had previously had in the United Kingdom. Before entry into the common market that might well have been predicted as the optimum commercial strategy.

With accession there was indeed an initial boom in foodstuff exports to Germany. Foodstuffs (SITC 0) made up 43.8 per cent of total Danish exports to the EEC in the first two years inside the common market. The sub-optimal aspect of trade with the EC partners, however, was how high the share of agricultural exports to the EC remained. In 1983 foodstuffs still made up 36 per cent of Denmark's total exports to the EC, compared to only 19.2 per cent of the value of its exports to the rest of the world. Germany did not become Denmark's biggest market for machinery exports, nor did the United Kingdom. Scandinavia remained more important.

The more rapid decline in the share of agricultural exports in total exports is one indicator that the pace of industrialisation was faster in Ireland than Denmark. A better one is the growth in the share of manu-factured goods in the value of total exports. Tables 2.10 and 2.11 compare for the two countries the relative shares in total export values of those two groupings of manufactured exports which grew most rapidly in world trade in the first three post-war decades, chemicals and chemical products (SITC 5) and machinery and transport equipment (SITC 7). It can be seen that machinery was already an important item in Danish exports in 1960 and one that grew rapidly in importance in the 1960s, following, at least in

Table 2.10 Exports of chemical products (SITC 5) as a percentage of total exports of Denmark and Ireland, 1960–88

	Denmark (%)	Ireland (%)
1960	4.19	0.56
1970	6.78	4.42
1980	7.28	12.59
1988	9.24	13.03

Source: OECD, Department of Economics and Statistics, *Foreign Trade by Commodities*, annual volumes.

Table 2.11 Exports of machines and transport equipment (SITC 7) as a percentage of total exports of Denmark and Ireland, 1960–88

	Denmark (%)	Ireland (%)
1960	18.53	3.96
1970	26.86	6.85
1980	24.07	18.48
1988	25.81	31.20

Source: OECD, Department of Economics and Statistics, *Foreign Trade by Commodities*, annual volumes.

that respect, the general trend of developed countries. In Ireland it was small and by 1970 still accounted for less than 7 per cent of total exports. It was during the 1970s that Irish exports of machinery began to catch up with similar Danish exports in their relative contribution to export earnings (Table 2.11). They were one of the dynamic elements in the Irish export boom of that decade (Table 2.8). By 1988 they contributed more than Ireland's earnings from agriculture. Exports of chemical products from Ireland in 1960 were insignificant (Table 2.10), but grew steadily as a share until 1980 when they comfortably surpassed those of Denmark in their relative contribution to export earnings (Table 2.11). They were, in fact, the biggest force in the first post-accession Irish export boom. By 1988 Irish exports were more industrial than Denmark's.

Ireland of course was growing in both cases from a much smaller industrial base than Denmark and spectacular percentage increases were for that reason easier to achieve. Nevertheless, it had become beyond dispute by 1988 an industrial country. The value of its total exports in 1960 was only 28.4 per cent of those of Denmark. The growth of manufactured exports meant that by 1988 its total exports were 70 per cent of those of Denmark. This is reflected in growth rates of national product. Real GDP grew in Ireland over the period 1973–9 at 4.9 per cent a year; in Denmark at 1.9 per cent.

Over the years 1979–89 it grew at 2.9 per cent in Ireland and at 1.8 per cent in Denmark. Over the whole period 1960–89 Ireland grew at 4.0 per cent a year, Denmark at 3.0 per cent.[34]

It is time to return to Sørensen's argument that Denmark deliberately restricted the potential growth of its manufacturing trade with Germany. She did not work out the statistical detail of her argument nor contemplate the possible economic consequences of Denmark's choice. Her interest was in explaining the inherent, domestic political logic of the strategy. Few, I suppose, now believe that the invisible hand alone decided the direction of trade flows within the common market before the 1990s. Sørensen's assertion, nevertheless, was a large one. It is, however, strengthened by the statistical evidence. It was through the interchange with Germany of industrial exports, and especially in the two groups of manufactures that are considered here, that the industrialisation of western Europe's less industrialised countries took place so rapidly after 1945 and Germany's role in that interchange remained, as we have seen, a constant of western Europe's economic history from then until the present day. The two significant exceptions have been, throughout, Denmark and Ireland. Ireland's exceptionalism is, however, an illusion. From the United Kingdom's entry into the European Community on the same day as its own, Ireland was able to follow in the 1970s the same commercial path to industrialisation as others had done earlier, but to do so through its connections to the British market, for after entry the United Kingdom played the subsidiary role to Germany in facilitating the same interchange of manufactures. As Irish governments after 1958 had come to think, trade with Britain was their bridge into the EEC and, as it turned out, the fast road to a successful industrialisation. Before British accession it seems to have been a rather slower road. Britain remained a much bigger market than Germany for Irish manufactured exports. For the two decades after entry, the rest of the EEC was also a bigger market than Germany. In that sense, Ireland achieved its goal of escape from the domination of the United Kingdom market and did so through industrialisation, not through agricultural trade. When Irish exports of machinery were very small in 1960, they were mostly to Britain. When they were substantial in 1988, less than a third were to Britain. By the 1980s a larger share of Ireland's engineering exports went to Germany than of Denmark's (Table 2.12).

If Denmark's persistence with engineering exports to Scandinavia rather than to Germany was a conscious choice, how was it made operative?

Was it a consensual national compromise between industrialists, government and trade unions, as Sørensen implied? Did this depend on trade union influence within the Social Democratic Party? Was it made operative through close intra-Scandinavian business links, cartels perhaps, which Danish business needed to do no more than preserve under an uninquisitive or a

Table 2.12 Geographical distribution of Danish and Irish exports of machines and transport equipment (SITC 7), 1960–88 (by % of their total value of exports in that category)

	1960		1970		1980		1988	
	Denmark	*Ireland*	*Denmark*	*Ireland*	*Denmark*	*Ireland*	*Denmark*	*Ireland*
To Germany*	9.82	9.74	9.76	7.20	14.66	19.71	13.73	15.77
To EEC	20.32	12.46	19.75	11.12	40.97	79.10	68.01	76.34
To United Kingdom	4.44	61.19	10.89	51.26	10.36	39.40	9.21	31.57
To Scandinavia**	28.75	1.94	25.76	4.16	21.42	5.87	21.40	5.79

Source: OECD, Department of Economics and Statistics, *Foreign Trade by Commodities*, annual volumes.

Notes

* German Federal Republic.

** In the case of Denmark, Scandinavia is Finland, Norway and Sweden. In the case of Ireland, it is Denmark, Finland, Norway and Sweden.

benevolent government eye? Or was there more active government oversight, perhaps through banks or other forms of pressure? Or was there simply no powerful motive to change the pattern allied to a general sentiment that it was as well not to?

Denmark's income per capita remained, after all, high by all European and world standards. A growth rate of national product of 3 per cent per year over thirty years was comfort indeed at such a level. Sweden and Switzerland recorded a lower rate, but nevertheless remained by per capita national income measurements among the world's five wealthiest countries. Ireland's experience of industrialisation was explosive, yet in the year the European trading system began to be more genuinely liberalised by the Single European Act, Danish exports were still almost a third greater in value than Ireland's. And perhaps we should take into account the problems that, in comparison, Denmark did not have. It was not troubled by an invasion of foreign firms whose linkages to the 'indigenous' economy were tenuous at best and more usually non-existent. It did not have to forfeit, as Ireland did, tax income from businesses. It did not have to make massive adjustments of employment within a manufacturing sector, the profitability of whose different parts changed dramatically over short periods of violent growth, as happened during Ireland's two great trade booms to the EEC. It did not have to anticipate and then witness the departure of 'non-indigenous' industries to places where wages were lower. The Danish welfare state, of which throughout this story the European Community was usually pictured in Denmark as an enemy, survived unscathed. It did not have much to cope with, by other European standards. The Irish welfare state only faintly existed.

It would be difficult, however, not to believe that there was some sacrifice of growth involved. Growth is income, in Denmark relatively equally distributed. When machinery was so prominent a sector of the Danish economy, and when it was in almost every western European country a rapidly growing, usually the most rapidly growing, sector of the industrial economy, when its growth was demonstrably increased by its linkages to the world's second biggest capital goods producer, Germany, there was surely a sacrifice in persisting with Sweden and Norway as the two largest markets, the surviving shadow of the elusive Nordek. Denmark needed no bridge to the common market, of which it was a small peninsula and some offshore islands. Its choice for Scandinavia was one of affinities, of language, culture, social attitudes and social policy, but it may well have been also a choice strengthened by suspicion of the EEC's corporatist capitalism and by a defensive nationalism against Germany. Ireland has had vigorous disputes with the European Community, but has remained a firm adherent of the Community's political procedures and structures. Denmark's suspicions of the Community

Table 2.13 Geographical distribution of Danish and Irish exports of chemical products (SITC 5), 1960–88 (by % of their total value of exports in that category)

| | 1960 | | 1970 | | 1980 | | 1988 | |
	Denmark	Ireland	Denmark	Ireland	Denmark	Ireland	Denmark	Ireland
To Germany*	7.76	7.46	10.02	8.76	10.02	7.77	9.02	7.45
To EEC	19.35	28.04	22.30	20.38	33.07	65.63	37.06	63.06
To United Kingdom	4.41	57.08	6.94	42.70	8.98	24.40	8.94	22.43
To Scandinavia**	22.30	0	28.55	0.96	22.43	1.91	21.51	3.19

Source: OECD, Department of Economics and Statistics, *Foreign Trade by Commodities*, annual volumes.

Notes
* German Federal Republic.
** In the case of Denmark, Scandinavia is Finland, Norway and Sweden. In the case of Ireland, it is Denmark, Finland, Norway and Sweden.

Table 2.14 Danish and Irish exports of chemical products (SITC 5) and machines and transport equipment (SITC 7) as a share (%) in total exports by value

	Denmark		Ireland	
	SITC 5	SITC 7	SITC 5	SITC 7
1960	4.19	18.53	0.56	3.96
1970	6.78	26.86	44.42	6.85
1980	7.28	24.10	6.51	18.48
1988	9.24	25.81	13.03	31.20

Source: OECD, Department of Economics and Statistics, *Foreign Trade by Commodities*, annual volumes.

have not been allayed, they have grown with membership. The child of the 1960s was father to the man.

It may be that in positioning itself safely as it had wished on a tripod of trade to Scandinavia, to the United Kingdom and to Germany, Denmark achieved safety rather than the shocks which can lead to dynamic growth. The European Council of Trades and Industries, a Danish association which financed part of the vote 'yes' campaign in the referendum of 1972 and helped to organise it, took as its newspaper campaign slogan 'Security – as we like it'. In retrospect that was indeed the outcome. Intra-Scandinavian trade was carefully preserved while the unadventurous, prosperously cushioned safety of the EC's Common Agricultural Policy, a soft touch for Denmark's efficient agriculture shaped as it had been to compete in open world markets, meant that gains to trade and perhaps to welfare were less from Denmark's accession to the European Community than they might have otherwise been. The search for security, brought to a happy conclusion in 1973, may have produced just that, because Denmark's political economy demanded no more.

3   Europe's Africa

The common market of the European Union does not derive its great commercial bargaining power solely from its domination of the trade among the countries of the European continent. It has a widespread network of trade agreements, with North African and Middle Eastern countries, with former Soviet Republics in Central Asia, with the association of South-East Asian Nations, with most Latin American countries, and with Mercosur. These treaties and agreements have sprung from the ability of the European Union to speak with one voice on questions of commercial policy and trade regulation, even when it has had the utmost difficulty in doing so in other areas of foreign policy.

Yet it is with a part of the world, sub-Saharan Africa, which makes only a marginal contribution to the volume of world trade, where the EU has had its largest, most comprehensive and most standardised network of trade treaties since the foundation of the common market. The four Lomé Conventions, which covered the period 1975–2000, saw the EU sign treaties with an increasing number of sub-Saharan African states. Caribbean and Pacific states were also included when they had been previously colonies of EU member-states. When the Lomé Conventions were superseded by the Cotonou Agreement, signed in June 2000, there were 78 states in the African, Caribbean and Pacific Group (ACP). They included every African state south of the Sahara, except that the Republic of South Africa, which had not been a signatory of the Lomé Conventions, was only 'conditionally' a member of the Cotonou Agreement. The Lomé Conventions provided for duty-free access to the common market for most of the manufactured exports of their African signatories, albeit in practice neither in unlimited quantity nor in unlimited value. They provided on the same terms for the products of tropical agriculture, although not for products of temperate agriculture included in the Common Agricultural Policy, which had to be the subject of separate bargaining. They provided an export stabilisation scheme (Stabex) to reduce the fluctuations in export earnings of these underdeveloped territories. They provided development aid through loans made by the European Investment Bank and through the European Development Fund (EDF), they provided technical expertise and they subsidised interest rates.

Yet, although in real terms the value of trade between the EU and its ACP 'partners' has grown, it has done so much less than trade with other areas, with the outcome that the African states have become increasingly marginalised within the vast flows of world commerce. If we calculate the contribution of ACP countries to the total current value of all EU trade, including cross-border trade within the EU, it amounted in 2000 to 1.53 per cent of the exports of EU member-states and to 1.71 per cent of all their imports. In the 1980s the comparable figures were for exports 2.9 per cent and for imports 3.1 per cent. This decline was in spite of the fact that the exports of the ACP countries were also beneficiaries of the EU's Generalised System of Preferences. Why has so much diplomatic effort been spent on so large an area of the world for so meagre an economic result?

It was frequently said in the 1960s that for the USA it was a convenient Cold War arrangement that Europe would look after the West's interests in Africa, leaving the USA to defend them where it mattered more. The reality however was that the United States throughout its history had had few economic contacts with Africa, most of them ephemeral, many of them unhappy, and that after 1945 it was European countries which determined the destiny of much of the African continent. Britain, France, Portugal and Belgium politically and militarily ruled through their colonies and protectorates over large areas of Africa's land mass. Their presence and influence stemmed from half a millennium of commercial interest there, intensified in the last third of the nineteenth century into direct political control.

The Second World War and the Cold War, it is true, increased the USA's perception of the North African littoral as a vital western interest. In 1960 36.4 per cent of public sector investment in Africa north of the Sahara came from the USA. But France's stake in North Africa was larger; the comparable share of investment from France was 54 per cent. South of the Sahara in the same year, however, French and British public sector investment amounted to almost 70 per cent of the total, US investment only to 6.4 per cent.[1]

In the immediate aftermath of the war politicians in Britain and France separately conceived grandly over-ambitious ideas of opening up rich sources of raw materials and food in Africa which would save on dollar expenditures and help in the longer term to restore the international payments position of their countries and to strengthen Europe against American power. The idea proved to be only another in a long line of beguiling dreams of Africa. Its sentiments, though, were indicative of a strong feeling that Africa had been brought into world commerce and developed by Europe and that the extent of its colonisation was so great that European nations must be the predominant influence on its development. This sentiment lingered when Washington in the 1960s perceived a threat of Communism in sub-Saharan Africa. By European states the USA was seen in Africa as more a rival than an ally. This was not a costly stance. Not many European troops were needed to prop up African regimes. Rarely were America's political or economic interests in Africa so strong as to lead it to oppose the actions of its allies there. More than one half of Africa's imports by value in the 1960s came from the EEC; between 7 and 10.5 per cent came from the USA, a proportion often exceeded by that of Asia, even when Japan is excluded from the calculation. Similarly, although the USA is more important to Africa as a market than a supplier, over half the value of African exports in most years after 1945 was directed to those countries which eventually constituted the expanded EC in 1973. Africa, in fact, has been a part of European commercial history for more than five hundred years and it is that which explains the EEC's predominance there after the Second World War.

It does not, however, entirely explain why the EC went to such pains to extend so large a network of trade treaties to a continent where it was not seriously challenged and with which the value of its foreign trade, in comparison with the rest of the world, was so small. Its trade with sub-Saharan Africa was, for example, less valuable than the trade of the EC member-states with Asia and would grow more slowly, in spite of the network of trade treaties, than the Asian trade. Within the globalised economic perspective which began to be opened up by the US/EEC negotiations in GATT in the 1970s, trade with Africa was of minor economic importance except for the trade in energy sources from the states of the Mediterranean littoral. In spite of this, the European Community/European Union has been an instrument of support to the European states' continuing involvement in Africa and Africa has been an inherent part of the expansion of United Europe's economic and political presence in the world.

Although the history of the European Community's expansion is almost entirely written as though it were a purely European event, in truth each expansion of the EC/EU except for that of 1981 has been a global event. As the historical accounts of the expansions rarely overstep the frontiers of Europe, nor does the political theory which seeks to explain them. Surely such a narrowing of our vision vitiates our understanding of post-war European history. We should understand the history and politics of the European Union as being also a part of the preservation of Europe's position and importance in the world, but the only context in which history or politics attempts such an understanding is in that of Europe's relationship with the USA, usually arriving at a tritely evasive Eurocentric conclusion that we are the Greeks of America's Roman Empire.

Within the text of the Treaty of Rome the EEC made provision for 'association' with seventeen African territories of its member-states, most of them former French or Belgian colonies in the course of changing their status. Association was 'primarily to further the interests and prosperity of the inhabitants of these countries and territories in order to lead them to the economic, social and cultural development to which they aspire'.[2] With one addition these countries were eventually all to become signatories of the Yaoundé Convention, signed in the capital of Cameroon in 1963. They took the collective title, Association des Etats Africains et Malgache (AEAM), in its English version after 1972 'Associated African States and Madagascar' (AASM).

This was done under French insistence, France holding up the signing of the Treaty of Rome until the other member-states agreed to finance part of the development costs of its empire and to do so within the formalised context of the treaty which was to lay the basis for a European Union. Similar arrangements were made for the Belgian Congo and for the Dutch Antilles. The member-states at first agreed to this only on a temporary, short-term basis, so that the continuation of these arrangements was not put on a permanent basis for a decade after the signing of the treaty. Germany and Italy had been deprived of their African empires as a result of the First and Second World Wars and were far from ready to commit themselves permanently to the financial support of French imperial ambitions as part of the price of a European Community.

Nevertheless, in continuing to insist that such financial support should become built into the EEC's permanent activities, eventually France achieved its goal of linking the future of the former French empire, for which various ideas for union with France filled the political air in Paris, with the vision of a Union of Europe. The Treaty of Rome, when signed in 1957, was seen by some political circles in France as the counterpart of a grand, francophone, worldwide union. The two unions should form two conjoint spheres of French economic and cultural dominance, on which post-war French foreign policy could be balanced. This insistence that the European Communities were not a retreat into Europe has survived, even though the road from the 1946 constitution of the Fourth Republic to the signing of the first Yaoundé Convention in 1963, which initiated the European Communities' trade treaties with sub-Saharan Africa, can be seen from a French perspective as a retreat.

The word used by French politicians to describe their African programme was 'association', a dynamic interchange between developed metropole and underdeveloped 'associated' territories or states which would provide a framework for more rapid economic and social development. In the early years of the European Economic Community, when France's influence in that institution was all-pervasive, the Community itself borrowed the concept, calling the commercial treaty which it signed with Greece in July 1961 a 'Treaty of Association'. In this case it had the specific meaning that Greece would be raised with the Community's help to a level of development where it would be able to become a member-state of the EEC.

For France in the 1950s, 'association' had a complex aura of meaning. It still embraced for some the concept of colonial empire as a process of 'assimilation', a gradual integration of colonial peoples into the norms of French cultural, social and political behaviour, a process whose difficulties had been all too painfully experienced in the inter-war period. For others, it replaced such characteristics of earlier attitudes to less 'evolved' societies, in order to adapt them more rapidly to a post-war world of increasing trade liberalisation and prosperity. Trade and aid combined would, in principle, increase the levels of development and income within the French overseas empire more rapidly than in the inter-war period and, for more conservative administrators, establish more speedily and widely French norms which had earlier been attained by only small elite colonial groups. Similarly, the EC raising the level of the Greek economy to the point where Greece could eventually enter the EEC without severe problems to either party to the treaty could be understood as a statement that Greece could become in economic, political and social respects worthy of assimilation into the Communities.

The political ideas which represented 'association' as a contemporary and more operable concept of 'assimilation' proved more a linguistic than a political adaptation to reality. Even by the time of the Treaty of Association between the EEC and Greece the word 'association' was shedding some of its aura of meaning as the French Union proved a concept too nebulous to produce a counterpart to the European Union. The Union was rejected by 'Indo-China', Morocco and Tunisia. It proved unimposable on Algeria, even though Algeria was constitutionally part of mainland France.

The Gaullist Fifth Republic, nevertheless, was linguistically explicit in replacing the failed French Union with the French Community and so keeping the idea of a double Community alive. The constitution of the French Community revealed, however, the narrow boundaries within which the Fifth Republic hoped to confine both Communities. The Executive Council of the French Community was made up of the Prime Minister of France, the heads of government of the member-states and the ministers in charge of 'common affairs'. 'Common affairs' were foreign policy, defence, economic policy and monetary policy. The ministers of common affairs were all French. The final court of arbitration was the French Supreme Court. In effect members of the French Community other than France itself had only autonomy in a limited area of domestic decision-making. Association turned out to mean a tie with France which could not be broken without incurring severe penalties. Independence was possible, but it meant leaving the French Community and forfeiting economic aid.

The constitution of the French Community and acceptance of membership within it was the subject of a referendum in each state. In sub-Saharan Africa only Guinea voted against membership, although in Niger the vote in favour was only 36.6 per cent. France began its departure from Guinea the following day, taking with it a considerable part of the infrastructure it had earlier provided, and tried unavailingly to delay, perhaps to prevent, the newly independent country's entry into the United Nations. For the Fifth Republic, as for the Fourth, the relationship with underdeveloped Africa had to be a tutelary one.

Yet in 1957 the future for West African states had already been set by the independence of Ghana, the former British colony of Gold Coast, followed by its acceptance of membership in the British Commonwealth. The concept of the British Commonwealth had also, in British eyes, a tutelary aspect, to serve as a prop and a guide to democratic government, of which the United Kingdom and other 'white' dominions would serve as examples. British governments were to be soon disappointed by the weakness of any tutelary impact of the constitutional paraphernalia of the Commonwealth on emancipated colonies and to wonder during the 1960s whether as an organisation it was worthwhile. It was to survive, even to recover, perhaps because of its less organic and tutelary aspect, longer than the French Community, whose Executive Council met for the first time on 3 February 1959 and for the last time on 21 March 1960.

Mali declared its independence from the French Community in September 1959, Madagascar shortly afterwards. In the course of 1960 the early view of President de Gaulle that the price of independence was secession from the French Community had to be replaced by the concept of independence in, to bring two concepts together, 'association' with the Community. In empirical terms this meant that the independence of French Community member-states, even when self-proclaimed, would be followed by cooperation agreements signed with the European Community. The substance of the agreements was that they were trade treaties. For former French Community members these agreements involved remaining in the franc zone for foreign trade settlements. The treaties were written as contractual mutual preference agreements to emphasise the concept of a francophone Africa maintaining close links with and being dependent on France and through France the European Community.

The final basis for a permanent financing of the European Community's own administrative resources was, however, only secured as part of an agreement by France, reached in December 1969 under pressure from the other member-states, that the European Community should open negotiations with the United Kingdom, Denmark, Ireland and Norway for accession. The levies which were imposed on intra-trade within the EEC on agricultural produce became one source of the permanent income of the EEC itself. This linkage of the Common Agricultural Policy to the provision of the European Commission's own permanent funding was to have significant consequences for African exports to Europe, for the Treaties of Association which were negotiated with the francophone African states and which made up the Yaoundé Convention of 1963 had exempted from free entry into the EEC all agricultural products which were subject to CAP regulations within the Community. Imported into the EEC they would pay the same levy as agricultural products crossing frontiers within the EEC. The duration of the Yaoundé Convention, four years, was determined by the period of time for which EC finance for the project was at that date guaranteed by France's partner states.

Because the first Yaoundé Convention was intended by Paris to save something of the concept of the French Community as a platform for French power and influence, to that end it seemed essential to sustain the juridical and economic principles of contractual mutuality between France and its former African colonies. The Yaoundé signatories must appear legally as an organic entity, although this could not strictly apply to the Belgian colonies nor to Cameroon and Togo. Even they, however, could not become, in French eyes, a mere part of the aid-receiving world on the same terms as other less developed countries.

To establish such an entity French governments thought it advantageous to conform to GATT rules. France did not have to search them too hard to find the principle that would sustain the idea of an organic entity. The GATT was all that remained of the post-war American proposal for an International Trade Organisation (ITO) which had been intended to enforce a non-discriminatory system of world trade on a multilateral basis which, in America's eyes, would drive down tariffs and remove quantitative restrictions. It failed to materialise because of the opposition of less developed countries and their demands for exceptional treatment. Some of the exceptions which the less developed wanted found their way into the GATT, which, intended as a preliminary agreement to the negotiation for the ITO, ended as all that was left of the American plans when the ITO failed to come into existence. It did contain phrases allowing less developed countries some scope for protecting infant industries by tariffs or to impose quantitative restrictions on imports to defend their balance of payments. Essentially, however, GATT was an instrument for regulating trade in manufactures between developed economies. It was only in 1958 that it first applied itself to studying whether the developed economies were hampering the growth of exports from the less developed. That they were doing so became in the 1960s a central aspect of the charge of 'neocolonialism' levied against the commercial policies of European countries towards their former dependencies. The GATT's own independently carried out survey indicated that there was some force to the complaints of the less developed.

The developed countries themselves, however, were divided on what should be done. The USA continued to insist on non-discrimination, the European Community on the need to accept discrimination in favour of the less developed. One American target was tariff preferences offered by the UK to British Commonwealth countries and by analogy preferences offered by the European Economic Community to former French Community members. It had been a cardinal point of US commercial policy that the United Kingdom should be barred from extending any new tariff preferences after 1945, especially for agricultural products from the Commonwealth which competed with equivalent US exports.

Preferences were, as part of the American idea of a post-war world trading system, to be steadily eliminated because they were a distortion of world trade in the interests of protecting regional trade when the true objective should be global trade. The EEC's foundation on the basis of implicit preferences between its member-states was allowable only under the GATT rule that the average height of its Common External Tariff was lower than that of its previous component parts. For the European Community, and particularly for France in the 1950s, preferences were seen as a way of favouring exports from underdeveloped states which were still the responsibility of France, the European Economic Community, and other member-states and on this point France and Britain did not differ. When the voices of the underdeveloped were added to this dispute, they too were mostly in favour of preferences. It was only two years after the first Yaoundé Convention that Part IV was added to the GATT agreement, encouraging preferential concessions to the underdeveloped. Part IV was not binding on GATT members; it was only permissive. It was, however, in conformity with the 1962 United Nations Conference on Trade and Development (UNCTAD) reporting the need for a more positive commercial policy towards the underdeveloped.

While preferences were the basis of French and EEC policy, the Yaoundé Convention of 1963 trod the path of political correctness by proclaiming itself a free trade area within Africa and thus, to deploy a useful German word, 'Gattkonform', because there would be 'free entry' among its African member-states. The fact that the level of intra-trade between the African signatories was very low did not invalidate the argument. It allowed the French to incorporate into the text of Yaoundé the concept of mutual preferences between an African free trade area and the European common market. In the event the EC allowed the African associates to take advantage of any aspect of any wording of any escape clauses in the treaties not to offer preferences. The reverse preferences, as the British called them, were a form of political symbolism. France preferred to call them 'reciprocity', for they preserved the idea of association in an organic entity.

The relationship of the United Kingdom to the European Economic Community's role in African trade arose on each occasion when the UK applied for membership. It was agreed in principle in 1961 at the time of Britain's first application to join the EEC that the British colonies and dominions in sub-Saharan Africa should be allowed to join on similar terms the Yaoundé Convention, although the Republic of South Africa was deemed a developed economy and thus excluded. In its Declaration of Intent in 1963, before the French veto fell on the British negotiations for entry, the Community made clear that various options, including that of a Treaty of Association, would be available to British Commonwealth African states on terms comparable to those of the first Yaoundé associates, irrespective of the success or failure of Britain's own negotiations. After the French veto on British entry, it was that offer which was to lead British East African states in the course of the 1960s towards seeking their own trading arrangements with the Community, although not a Treaty of Association, and Mauritius, which had as good a claim to being francophone as anglophone, to sign a Treaty of Association and in the second Yaoundé Convention join the AEAM countries.

At the time of Britain's second membership application in 1967 it had been made clear by the Foreign Secretary, George Brown, that former British territories in Africa which wanted to sign agreements with the Community were free to do so, a statement repeated by the Chancellor of the Exchequer, Anthony Barber, in Luxembourg at the end of June 1970. The Belgian Foreign Minister, Pierre Harmel, in response to Barber's statement, indicated that any country which asked to join the EC would have to accept Yaoundé as part of the *acquis communautaire*.

The first Yaoundé Convention expired at the end of May 1969. The second Convention was signed on 29 July 1970, to take effect from the start of 1971. The Hague summit meeting of the heads of state of the EC member-states in December 1969 had decided to open negotiations with the United Kingdom in respect of its application for membership of the European Community. Those negotiations by the close of 1971 had reached a point where British accession looked probable. If it came about, the new entrants to the European Community would become members on 1 January 1973 and a third Yaoundé Convention would be negotiated to start operations in 1975. If Commonwealth countries accepted the Convention, there would be a freeze of trading rules and conditions until 1975. Harmel's statement indicated that, at least as far as France and Belgium were considered, unfreezing the rules would not mean changing them in any important way.

The organic entity that France had sought to build was now faced with housing a much more populous set of African states, some of them more developed than their francophone counterparts, all of them to varying degrees anglophone, most of them inspired by the British model of seeking trade and income wherever it was to be found and not necessarily solely with the metropole, and one of them, Nigeria, whose foreign trade and political influence were on an altogether different scale from the others. France's internal discussion about whether Nigeria should be allowed to sign Yaoundé was not positively resolved until summer 1973. Nevertheless, French officials hoped that British entry would help to cement the European position in Africa and provide substantial financial help towards African economic development. It was, in fact, assumed from the outset of negotiations on the British side that the UK would pay an equivalent contribution to France towards aid for the Yaoundé countries. Politically, British officials took the view that a Franco-British agreement to maintain in common the structure of Yaoundé would be advantageous to both powers.

This display of unity and readiness to accept the burden of conformity in handling a common enterprise went as far as standing up to American objections to the expansion of the preferential trading system. The exact origins of the sudden American protest, made on the last day of 1970 by a visit from the Economic Counsellor at the American embassy in London, acting under orders from his government, to F.G.K. Gallagher, the Superintending Under-Secretary of the Trade Policy Department of the Foreign and Commonwealth Office, are hard to pin down. The prime minister had been told on 26 November 1970 by Mitchell Sharp, the Canadian Secretary of External Affairs that he 'wondered if there was going to be a great transformation in political terms' and gave as an example 'the far-searching effect of the EEC, its pull upon the Caribbean'.[3] United Kingdom insistence on incorporating the Caribbean and Pacific Commonwealth members and dependent territories into the Yaoundé structure had been accepted in France, at first somewhat reluctantly, although the proposal envisaged integrating French Pacific and Caribbean islands also. In subsequent British discussions with Germany it was to emerge that Germany wished to keep its distance from extending the range of the Yaoundé agreements beyond Africa and the Indian Ocean because it would be seen as a challenge in areas where American trade interests predominated.

It is possible that it was the apprehension about the Community's extension of its trade treaty network to the Caribbean which sparked the American protest which kept diplomats busy on New Year's Day 1971, but it is more likely that it was made with an eye to future negotiations in GATT to try to win some concessions there in return for withdrawing their objection. In delivering his government's protest the Economic Counsellor lumped together Commonwealth African and Caribbean countries as countries to which the US Administration 'had strong objections to the offer of associate status' on the grounds that association would enlarge an already discriminatory trading bloc and would be a backward step in the liberalisation of world trade.[4] Washington would regard any such arrangement as contrary to articles I and XXIV of GATT.

Well might British diplomats have been startled to discover that after following American encouragement to join the European Communities they were now to be strongly discouraged from pursuing international trade arrangements which had not been at all discouraged in 1961 or 1967. Under questioning, US officials seemed to be hinting that this disruptive intervention was a bargaining counter to obtain concessions from the Common Agricultural Policy regime in favour of their own agricultural exports. The extent and nature of these concessions was not specified, nor whether the problem as seen in Washington was Europe's protection of its own farmers or the lesser threat of direct competition between preferential tropical agricultural exports to Europe and similar American exports. Given the intensity of the struggle in GATT over the CAP's protection of the Community's farming sector and its subsidisation of the export of surpluses in the 1970s it seemed more likely that this was the issue at stake.

Sir Con O'Neill, the Foreign and Commonwealth Office official who steered the UK's negotiating tactics in its application to join the EEC, told the US embassy officials that 'he thought they should now reflect whether they were not putting at risk the conclusion of another treaty'.[5] In fact the USA had made a similar protest to other member-states of the Community and to the European Commission. There was no hint of any British retreat from the position they had taken up. The issue was inserted into a meeting between Edward Heath and the European Commissioner and former French Foreign Office official Jean-François Deniau, head of DG-8 (Development). Deniau had not been surprised by the American initiative, for he supposed that there would eventually have to be some form of association with the Community for all western European countries who were not member-states as well as for the British Commonwealth countries in Africa and the Caribbean, so that the number of countries with some form of Community preference would rise to more than sixty. It was this vision, he thought, that had strengthened the US Department of Agriculture's hand sufficiently to force the President to adopt a less welcoming attitude to the Community's role.

Heath was not the man to change his negotiating tactics in the project which dominated his term of office, as it had dominated his earlier ministerial experience, to suit small shifts of power in the White House.

The Prime Minister and M. Deniau agreed that American fears on this matter were highly one sided: the United States government was not deeply engaged in a political sense in Africa, and did not take account of the cost to Britain and the Community of support for developing countries in Africa. This whole subject was one on which Britain and the Community would need to have a common front.[6]

This agreed, forth they went together.

In the event the twenty-one signatories of Yaoundé-2 were to be joined by twenty-six more countries, including Caribbean and Pacific mini-states, both francophone and anglophone. Hence they were known as the ACP (African, Caribbean and Pacific countries). The new agreement was not signed in Yaoundé but, appropriately, in Lomé, the capital of Togo which had a history of both French and British administration. Known as the Lomé Convention, or Lomé-1, it began at the start of 1975 for a five-year term accompanied by a certain amount of favourable propaganda to emphasise that it was a new deal for Africa which would remedy the more strongly criticised aspects of Yaoundé.

In general economists have not shared the view of the Lomé Conventions as a new deal. They have seen it rather as the continuation of a framework which made insufficient and inappropriate provision for development in Africa. The wider argument supporting this view arises from the persistence of Africa's problems, poverty and its accompaniment, hunger and AIDS. A narrower view would refer to the low level and value of the exports of the African signatories of the Lomé Conventions. This narrower perspective also, however, leads into the issue of whether investment has been sufficient or well-directed. The issues raised by the length of time over which the Lomé Conventions operated raise other and wider political questions as well. These questions apply to the whole span of the Lomé Conventions.

Lomé-2 ran from 1980 to 1985, Lomé-3 from 1985 to 1989 and Lomé-4 throughout the following decade. By 2000 Deniau's forecast of the number of countries that would have Treaties of Association with the EC had been comfortably exceeded by those in the Lomé system alone. The last Convention covered sixty-nine ACP countries. Each successive Convention tinkered with the rules to meet a certain amount of the criticism of the earlier one, but not so that the criticism was ever stilled. It is almost impossible to find any author ready to claim that either the Yaoundé or Lomé Conventions satisfactorily fulfilled the aims publicly proclaimed for them in the Treaty of Rome.

Since all the Conventions were formal trade agreements, it is understandable that the most frequent criticism of them was their failure to increase Africa's role in European trade. To disburse aid without creating more trade invites all the criticisms of charity and suggests, also, that the aid was ill-placed. The first two years of Lomé-1 did generate an increase in real values of exports from the signatory countries to the EC. Each European expansion of the EC, however, was likely to produce such a result by itself. The first expansion, for example, did result in an increase of Danish and Irish imports, previously almost non-existent, from Africa. In 1977, however, the total real value of the exports of the African signatories to the European Community was lower than before the Convention was signed. This fall in real terms was accompanied by a persistent growth in the relative value of exports to Europe from other, non-Lomé, developing countries, mainly in Asia.

The relatively poor performance of Europe's economies after 1972 culminated in the 1979 recession, the same year that Lomé-2 was being negotiated. In many EEC countries the impact of manufactured imports from less-developed countries was claimed to be an important factor in the recession. Although non-Community textile imports into the four biggest EC economies in 1977 were only about 5.3 per cent of the total value of OECD manufactured exports in that year, a lower share than in 1963, they were blamed as contributory to the recession. In so far as OECD economies in general, and EEC economies in particular, were concerned they were not in fact facing competition from less developed economies so much as from the more developed next-industrialising countries. Quantitative restrictions on imports of yarn and textiles into the EC nevertheless were aimed at restricting African exports as well as Mexican or Korean and were rationalised by the end of the 1970s into the Multifibre Arrangement. To a certain extent the EC was influenced in these policies by its expansions to include Greece and then Spain and Portugal. It was offering an open market to three new European members whose textile and footwear manufacturing and exporting had grown rapidly in the 1960s. Internationalising quantitative restrictions on textiles by way of the Multifibre Arrangement made it more difficult to place the ACP countries under a less restrictive set of rules.

The negotiations for and the signing ceremony of Lomé-2 were not happy events. The ACP countries unsuccessfully pursued a claim for exemption from quantitative restrictions on imports of goods which, although they had been important to the first stages of industrialisation in European countries, were now, as the ACP countries rightly argued, no longer in the vanguard of technological development. The EC made just enough concessions to stop them breaking off the negotiations. Several, including Nigeria, had seriously considered doing so. By the opening date of Lomé-4 almost all manufactured exports from the African signatories were, as far as tariffs were concerned, exempt from the Common External Tariff of the EC/EU. However, the non-tariff barriers placed in their way meant that their real values had stagnated.

For agricultural products the condition was maintained from the outset that the Conventions could not apply to products covered by the terms of the Community's Common Agricultural Policy. This was extended to horti-culture, so that certain African crops, such as strawberries, were seen as undesirable competition with the Community's own production. More bizarrely for the annals of protectionism, the same ruling was applied to bananas. Other African crops were subject to worldwide cartel management which regulated the quantities which could be exported to the EEC, imposing a ceiling on them. Of these, sugar was the most extensively grown. Lomé-1 would not have come into force without a separate agreement between Britain, France and the EEC to integrate their own worldwide policies on sugar and banana importing, which involved a fiercely disputed concession to Germany to allow it to continue to import bananas from Central America. Beet sugar was a temperate zone crop whose output European countries had to balance against the need to sustain exports of cane sugar from tropical former colonies, some of which in the Caribbean and the Pacific had almost monocultural agricultural sectors. In short, there was no free international market for areas of tropical agricultural output which clashed with the output of rival products in Europe.

It was not only crops which fell under quantitative restrictions. Beef exports to Britain from cattle-rearing economies like Botswana proved a subject for hard bargaining between Britain and the EC. The share of sub-Saharan African states in the agricultural imports of the EC by value fell from 6 per cent in 1976 to 4.4 per cent in 1990 and to 3.2 per cent in 1992. While this was more a function of increased imports from elsewhere than of a fall in imports from the African states of Lomé it hardly merited the word 'partnership' repeatedly used to justify the Conventions.

At the same time Africa's markets remained dominated by Europe's exports. Western Europe (the EC plus other non-centrally planned European economies) was responsible for 67 per cent by value of world exports to Africa in 1980. Japan had the second largest share with only 9 per cent.[7]

How may we explain this outcome? A not unusual explanation is that Africa has little or nothing to export except agricultural products, which faced many barriers. Oil has been a notable exception, but on a large scale only for Nigeria. Other than oil, certain of the rarer mineral ores found a steady market in Europe, although often tied to one particular manufacturing company there. Manufacturing industry mostly produced for the domestic market. But this can be no final explanation, for such could have been written about most European economies in the early nineteenth century. If it is remarkable how little the commodity structure of African exports altered over the thirty years of the Lomé regime, this must be also a comment about foreign markets for goods and foreign suppliers of capital, European markets and European investors.

Has Europe been mainly to blame for the outcome of its own grand project? Alternatively, is Africa to blame for its own stagnation? Corruption, tyranny, cynical regimes more interested in enriching themselves than their people, inefficient administration, inadequate education and the shortage of administrative talent that allows inefficient administration to persist; all these are cited as African states are now condemned to the ultimate indignity of being classified as 'failed states'.

It is evident that around and beyond the criticisms of the EC's trade regime, the European Community was dealing with enormous political problems for which the remedies exceeded its resources and its wits. It was not for helping the process of state-building in Africa that it had been created. That was the task of the governments of its member-states, one of the many areas of foreign policy where the involvement of some was greater than others.

One of the most widespread criticisms of the EC/EU is that its inability to act in common reflected a common political attitude to Africa, the continuation of 'colonialism' in a supranational cloak. But any explanation that assumes an unchanging situation is invalidated by the fact that the world's trading regime has been in a process of continual change towards liberalisation since Lomé-1 was signed. Lomé-1 itself was a fundamental change in the rules of trade from those governing Yaoundé-2.

If Britain and France went forth together they were soon to find themselves in serious disagreement over the path to take. French expectations that the UK would simply accept all the existing rules were soon shattered, revealing the wide gap that existed between their perceptions of the way Africa should be fitted into a more liberalised world trading system. From that dispute onwards many of Africa's political problems have been related to the impact of a worldwide and increasingly non-colonial framework for trade on its diverse societies and governments.

When British officials considered the rules of Yaoundé they were bound to ask whether the trade of African Commonwealth countries with the European Community should be within the same formula of an organic entity with mutual preferential obligations as metropolitan France had established with the former French Community. These arrangements had led, as France had intended, to the preservation and in some measure the subsidisation of French trade with its former African colonies under a set of conditions which meant that most of it remained confined to bilateral commercial exchanges with the metropole. This did not mean lower raw material prices for French processors, often the prices were much higher than prices paid for similar raw materials by British importers from British Commonwealth Africa, but it guaranteed a greater security of supply and preserved the organic entity of the franc zone and of a French cultural and political identity beyond France. The relative exclusivity of French trade with francophone Africa before Lomé-1 seems to have been considered as unthreatened except for the one major difficulty; Nigeria, so several French officials thought, was too big and too powerful to accept such arrangements without wishing to change them and perhaps dominate them. The issue of whether Nigeria should or should not be included in Lomé-1 was made even more troublesome by its own indecision. After it was included, Nigeria was responsible over the period 1976–8 for 28.9 per cent of the value of total EC imports from the ACP states.[8]

Britain had little interest in preserving a *chasse gardée* parallel to that of France in Africa. Its diplomats agreed that common action in Africa between the two countries would strengthen the position of both. But within the Foreign and Commonwealth Office the Overseas Development Administration saw its task as promoting the increase of worldwide trade. The value of British exports to and imports from Africa (minus industrialised South Africa) was less than the value of exports to and exports from Asia (minus industrialised Japan). Furthermore, trade with less developed Asia was growing more rapidly than with less developed Africa. The trading privileges of the small British colony of Hong Kong created more difficulties in the negotiations to join the European Community, because of its rapidly growing textile and footwear exports, than did the agreement, which only confirmed the earlier agreements, that there should be a common regime for African trade.

If we compare the geographical distribution of British and EEC trade in 1961–3, the period of Britain's first, failed negotiations for entry, we can see that this difference was already present then, although there was as yet no such administrative unit as the Overseas Development Administration. Exports from underdeveloped Asia to the EEC were little more than a third of their value to Britain and were a smaller share of total imports. When John Robertson, the head of the Foreign and Commonwealth Office's Department of European Integration attended in 1973 the second meeting of a new Cabinet Committee on EEC Relations with Developing Countries, set up to prepare British policy positions for the 'High Level Group' which the EC had constituted as a forum in which to reach an Anglo–French agreement on what would succeed Yaoundé-2, he was given a plain message by the Overseas Development Administration. Its own policy in Africa was to relate development aid to the principle of 'need', the least developed should receive more than the less developed, but the overall distribution of aid by the EC should be altered so as to 'secure some redirection of total aid from other EEC members to countries which would not be linked to the Community by association agreements and in which we had a major political and commercial interest. If this objective could not be secured, a disproportionate level of Community aid would go to countries in Africa and the Caribbean.'[9] Ways of doing this, perhaps by constituting a separate European Development Fund for non-associates, perhaps by extending the scope and powers of the European Development Fund itself to cover non-associates parallel to the one which was to be created for the associates, were discussed in the committee and ministers were asked to decide how best to implement such a policy. 'Worldwide trade' would thus mean as far as possible proportionately less money from the European Community for African and more for developing Asian countries. Ten days later it was laid down that 'Our own major objective in the work of the High Level Group was to secure an increased flow of aid from the Community countries to Asia.'[10]

Given this attitude, it was obvious that the European Integration Department would have little scope for going any further in its commitment to France than the decision made before negotiations for accession began that the UK payment for the costs of EC aid to Africa should be equal to the size of the French contribution and that they would be the two biggest contributors. The negotiations had reached agreement that the Commission's procedure suggested at the time of the 1967 application could be the basis for inviting African Commonwealth states to sign Treaties of Association. The states would be given three options: to sign a Treaty of Association like those of the Yaoundé Convention states; to sign a treaty of the type that had been signed by the countries of the Mediterranean littoral guaranteeing them some preferences in Community markets but without the special status of 'association'; to negotiate whatever individual terms they could with the EEC. The first option implied the acceptance of the reverse preferences signifying their membership of the mutual contractual regime which France insisted would demarcate them from the general body of states with which the EU had signed trade treaties.

It was only in November 1972 that the UK government concluded that association was the best option and found itself facing a dilemma which had never troubled the French. How could the United Kingdom recommend a course of action to newly and proudly independent countries? It had to use the help of German, Dutch and Italian diplomats to find out what options the new African Commonwealth countries were contemplating taking up. Even more difficult, would the Commonwealth states accept an option which meant offering reverse preferences to the EEC when their preferential trading relationship with Britain had embodied no such rule? The optimum solution therefore was that the Commonwealth countries should sign up for the new Lomé Convention, but reject the condition of 'reciprocity'. Preferences on EC markets would remain, but would not have to be offered to the EC.

At the time of the Lomé-1 negotiations the USA was struggling to bring to birth a Generalised Preference System for all less developed territories, but threatening to exclude from those preferences the exports of Caribbean countries which would be covered by Lomé preferences, on the grounds that those countries would be liable under the Lomé treaties to themselves provide preferences to European exporters. The issue was tackled at the highest level by Prime Minister Heath on the occasion of his visit to Washington in January 1973.[11] This at least had the effect of increasing the complications of any American preference scheme before Congress and played its part in delaying for much longer the establishment of an American generalised preference scheme. Edward Heath's action showed the British desire, in spite of all the difficulties, to reach agreement with France about a new convention for Africa to mark the beginning of one aspect of the European Community in which Britain was not an awkward partner. From its accession, the United Kingdom supported the EC in all issues to do with tariff bargaining. One purpose of British accession was to put the Community on a level of equal power with the USA in international trade disputes.

British anxieties about 'reciprocity' were treated by some French officials as a breach of the implicit promise after the summit in The Hague that the United Kingdom would accept in its entirety the *acquis communautaire*, but an *acquis* which had so many exceptions as the Yaoundé Conventions could scarcely be placed on the same footing as the Common Agricultural Policy. In discussions with the British Minister for Overseas Development, Richard Wood, and the Chancellor of the Duchy of Lancaster, John Davies, Claude Cheysson, who succeeded Deniau in 1973 as the European Commissioner for Development, argued that 'geographical limitation of association meant that association should have a contractual basis; albeit one which cost the developing countries nothing'. Davies gave the British answer, that aid should be on a worldwide basis and that an aid club for Africa would be 'dangerous'.[12] What probably lay behind the French insistence surfaced only at the end of the meeting, when Cheysson concluded that 'the main point was that it would be impossible to resist pressure to extend unreciprocated free entry to the EEC to the rest of the world'.[13] Preferences on the European market for African states would in effect be eroded by the spread of generalised preference schemes and the decline of tariffs. What then would distinguish Europe's Africa from the rest of the underdeveloped world, a helpless boat in a sea of globalised trade?

From early 1973 until the terms of Lomé-1 were settled in October 1974 France and Britain were at loggerheads over the issue of 'reciprocity'. The French desire to distinguish Africa as a continent for which Europe must proclaim a special responsibility, different conceptions of the limitations that should be placed on the globalisation of trade, the future of the French language in the world, the decision-making process inside the Community and money were all matters of dispute. The resolution of these disputes imposed limitations on the European Community's programme for Africa which were built into the Lomé regime for the next quarter of a century and could not be overcome.

The underlying problem was French insistence on maintaining the 'reciprocity' which had characterised the Yaoundé treaties as the basis of the future agreement. Their arguments for insisting on 'reciprocity' were nebulous and as D.J.E. Ratford of the European Integration Department was told by one of his officials after a conversation with the First Secretary of the French Embassy in London, Jean-Pierre Lafon, were expressed 'in a very theological way'.[14] The theology can be summed up as an insistence on mutual contractual obligations, sometimes said to be, as by Lafon, because only with such written obligations could Africa negotiate as an equal with Europe, sometimes said to be to maintain a legal and moral framework which went beyond the boundaries of mere commercial relationships. Léopold Senghor, President of Sénégal and until 1959 a deputy in the French National Assembly, while supporting both these views in meetings and speeches in Africa on behalf of French government policy, put a third slant on them. It was necessary, he seems to have believed, to maintain the contractual relationship of Yaoundé because it was essential that Africa should become 'Europeanised'. Left to the open winds of international commerce it might fall under the undesirable influence of another continent.

By other EC member-states, and particularly by German and Italian diplomats, the real reasons for the French insistence on reverse preferences were thought to be the pursuit of France's own economic interest in Africa, a way of ensuring that German and Italian trade would not displace old-established French business in Africa. As things stood, so Alessandro Grandi, head of the Italian Foreign Office's Department of External Relations with the Community, told the British Ambassador to Italy, 'the Yaoundé system, as it now operated, was little more than a way of preserving a French sphere of influence at Community expense'. Italy did not get its fair share of public contracts and 'had to content themselves with odds and ends which the French did not want'.[15]

Confronted with the argument that 'reciprocity' was fundamental to the acceptance by GATT of a new convention as a free trade area and thus to the continuation of preferences, British officials swept it aside by insisting that it would be easy to get a waiver from GATT which would allow the preferences to be maintained. It is noticeable, however, that they never produced any convincing plan or argument which would be presented to GATT and result in a waiver, even when challenged to do so by the European Commission.[16] Any such proposal would have had to win support from the USA and, because the USA had not yet withdrawn its opposition to extending preferences in the expansion of Yaoundé, that might mean a bargain which touched more closely the overall economic interests of the EEC. The USA might demand concessions from the CAP or, equally difficult, demand a larger share in the internationally regulated world trade in those agricultural products, sugar for example, which both France and Britain thought were more vital issues than a common European Community aid programme for Africa. How to get a waiver was, as Heath was feebly briefed by his officials to tell Cheysson, only 'a second priority', not 'something which we need to consider in detail now'.[17] What is more, the arguments of British officials, passed on to Heath to hold in reserve for possible use against Cheysson, told against that optimism. 'There is', they minuted, 'no evidence that third countries would be interested in negotiating concessions to the associables or the associated states in return for being treated on an equal basis with the EEC in their markets'.[18]

Heath and Pompidou, meeting in Paris on 21–22 May 1973, agreed that they had a major interest in continuing the Yaoundé arrangements. That Heath, as the minutes record, 'showed understanding' of the importance France attached to 'reverse preferences' did not weaken Britain's stance. This may have been related to Pompidou's final remarks about those preferences 'that they were not to be regarded as an exclusive privilege'.[19] By the date of that meeting, other meetings between anglophone and francophone African states seemed to be indicating that the francophone states were divided on the question of 'reciprocity' and not because of British intervention in their negotiations.

In February 1973 the French Foreign Ministry had decided to adopt something closer to the British position. It would recommend to ministers that 'reciprocity' would not be obligatory but could be maintained by those countries wishing to maintain it. This had been rejected by French ministers and it is in that light too that the evasive treatment of the issue by Heath and Pompidou should be seen. The Committee of Permanent Representatives in Brussels and the Council of Ministers were also divided over the issue. Belgium, Luxembourg and Ireland supported the French view; Germany, Italy, the Netherlands and Denmark supported that of the United Kingdom.[20] While Senghor campaigned in Africa for the status quo, everyone was awaiting the African voice.

The acknowledgement on both sides that they disagreed about the future terms of association and that those terms were not entirely theirs to settle cleared the way, however, for Franco–British agreement on related issues. Talks in London between John Robinson and Pierre Achard, Secretary General of the Comité Interministeriel pour les Questions de Coopération Economique Européenne, the Quai d'Orsay's policy-making centre for

Europe, on 7 April determined fundamental issues of Anglo-French joint action in Africa while leaving the question of reverse preferences in abeyance.

The French fear that, even were they to win the argument over 'reciprocity', the spread of generalised preference schemes would still eliminate the value of the Yaoundé preferences, increased the urgency to reach agreement with Britain on the specific modalities of trade in commodities already regulated by cartel arrangements. This, said Achard, would add more cement, good news to the ears of British officials who had also already decided that 'commodities' were the more important issue.

Second, accepting that 'commodities' were an issue which went beyond the scope of the EC and accepting perhaps also that they might well not reach an agreement about 'reciprocity', they agreed on limiting that part of the aid budget for Africa which would be disbursed by the European Community. Most aid for Africa would in future continue to be allocated and directed separately through bilateral agreements by the national governments in Paris and London. Under Lomé-1 only about 12.5 per cent of aid to the ACP countries was disbursed by the European Development Fund of the European Community and this figure remained more or less the same until the Lomé regime came to an end. In further talks in May the same two officials agreed to aim towards including Ethiopia, Liberia and Sudan in the new convention.[21]

The relative ease with which these agreements were reached is discussed below, but Britain and France still differed on the question of whether only states which were prepared to declare in advance that they accepted full association, Yaoundé-style, should be invited to negotiate. The speed with which agreement was sketched out on the other issues suggests that France was confident of retaining the Yaoundé model with 'reciprocity'. Other British officials began to suggest to the European Integration Department that it was time to give way. G.R. Denman wrote from the Department of Trade and Industry as early as 14 March that, unless the Commonwealth states were prepared to accept 'the principle of tariff reciprocity, in the very watered-down form in which it appears in the present Yaoundé arrangement, they are very unlikely to get to the negotiating table at all'.[22] By 25 May the UK Representative to the Community, Michael Palliser, was despairing of the EC member-states agreeing to open full negotiations on the due date unless those negotiations were confined to states which accepted beforehand the option of a Treaty of Association. He was asking how far he should retreat.[23] Nothing could prevent the continuation of reverse preferences, and with them perhaps the collapse of the idea of a Common European Community action in Africa, other than a switch by the Africans themselves to the position increasingly taken up by the Commonwealth states that 'reciprocity' was the unacceptable face of 'colonialism', a denial of their independence.

In defiance of the general view of British and French officials that Africans were incapable of reaching agreement on a common position in any international organisation, British policy was in the event rescued not by British officials but by agreement among Africans. A group of experts from the anglophone 'associables' met in Accra on 10–15 February 1973, without any accurate account of this discussion reaching British officials for about a month. The 'associables' then staged a meeting of political leaders in Nairobi on 6 April. They met with politicians from the Yaoundé countries at Abidjan on 12 April. Everything next moved to a full-scale meeting between 'associable' anglophone countries and existing Yaoundé associates at Abidjan on 9–13 May. There were no British or French officials or diplomats present at that last meeting, perhaps no white faces at all. With four dissentient countries, two, Ivory Coast and Sénégal, afterwards continuing to dissent, they agreed to nominate three spokesmen, one for Africa, one for the Caribbean, and one for the Pacific countries, to report their conclusions to the European Commission in Brussels on 25/26 July. They were Wenike Briggs (Minister of Trade for Nigeria), Shridath Ramphal (Foreign Minister of Guyana) and Sir Kamisese Ratumasu (Prime Minister of Fiji). Their reports, to the immense relief of the British officials present, and especially to Palliser, constituted to use Palliser's word, an 'onslaught' on the concept of reverse preferences.

It is worth citing Palliser's impressions at length, however, because they indicate that more was at stake than trade. He wrote:

> This was an extraordinary conference in the literal sense of the word. On a number of occasions over the past year, I have been struck by the sense of change that enlargement was bringing to the Community. But in some ways this week's conference was even more radical in its sense of change and in the mood of exhilaration at that change which one detected in the conference chamber. This must have been the first meeting ever held by the Community at which no single word of French was spoken from start to finish. The Danish President of the Council[24] made his formal speeches in Danish but conducted the conference in English. And it was in various types of English, the guttural West African of Mr Briggs, the lilting nasal Caribbean of Ramphal or the stalwart Oxford English of the Fijian Prime Minister, that these regional spokesmen expressed their views. The significance of this, in terms of the changed balance in the Community's relationship with its former colonial territories can have been lost on no-one: and was certainly not lost on the French. M. Deniau's face was a study in growing dejection as the conference proceeded: and not only because French ideas on reciprocity were being so soundly trounced.[25]

At stake also were France's hitherto unshakable domination of the European Community's decision-making machinery; the domination of the French language within the Community and its place in the wider world; the acceptance by former member-states of the French Community of French commercial policy; France's hope that organic ties with its former empire would prove a much greater reinforcement in French worldwide diplomacy than the anarchical freedom of views inside the Commonwealth; and, perhaps most important of all, France's ability to shape the rules of future globalisation of commerce.

The three reports could not lead to a decision. That had to await a plenary meeting. Over that period of waiting France's position on 'reciprocity' hardened to the point of refusing to countenance the possibility of any alternative, so that a stiff fight remained for British diplomats. Nevertheless, the three reports had fatally weakened France's support within the EC. What would be the point of insisting on a framework for future trade with the underdeveloped world which had been officially rejected by all but the two countries, France and Belgium, which continued to speak loudly for reverse preferences? France had been forced to hear the wider world speaking with its own voice and not through the mouths of French officials or a colonial elite. Palliser's sense of a moment of historical change was not self-indulgence.

Even so, it presented dangers to the United Kingdom. The British did not want to overthrow France's position in the Community; they wanted to share it. As Palliser concluded his account, 'in the long run our interests here are fundamentally the same as those of the French and of our other Community partners'.[26] The seeming victory over reverse preferences should be taken, he argued, as a signal to offer more concessions to French self-esteem in the negotiations about commodities than had been envisaged.

The question mark placed over the future of the French language in the European Community had given President Pompidou much concern throughout the negotiations for expansion, even to the point where Heath had assured him in spring 1971 that Britain would embark on a programme of improving the nation's ability to speak French. A group of distinguished literary personalities had published a letter to Pompidou asking him to ensure that 'French shared with English the privilege of being a universal language not only because of its cultural virtues but also because it is in practice the working language of Europe, as well as being the official language of the African states associated with Europe and where its use is indispensable.' The letter asked that French be recognised as the 'working language of an enlarged Europe'.[27] Pompidou did not go so far as to agree to that, wisely because the 25–26 July meeting in Brussels would have been an early demonstration of its impossibility as a goal. Heath's programme for enhancing French language-learning in Britain got little further than regular joint meetings of junior British and French civil servants. Globalisation of trade rules was to be accompanied by an increasing globalisation of the English language in international organisations, not, however, ascribable to Britain's importance.

Notice of change it clearly was. But the change did not consist solely of the entry into the European Community of another large economy with a different perspective on world trade. It was the Africans, Caribbeans and politicians from the Pacific who forced the change and did so for themselves. They would probably not have done so without having the Commonwealth states to strengthen their will in their councils, although the United Kingdom's direct influence on those states was tenuous and its effect uncertain. The European Community had entered the world, as well as the United Kingdom entering the Community. On those grounds alone it was a misleading verdict to call the event a British victory. It was also misleading because even in the autumn of 1973 French officials were still unwilling to have the Lomé Convention written differently from Yaoundé. Their only firm supporter by then however was Belgium, so that one might argue that the French domination of Commission decisions had also ended as an institutional norm, although in the years that followed that particular outcome was as ascribable to Germany as to Britain.

In so far as it was an economic victory, an assertion of British (or in French usage 'Anglo-Saxon') principles for the future international commercial policies of the European Communities, it was achieved by emboldening the future signatories of Lomé to believe that the world was all before them, where to choose their place of rest, and Providence their guide. As I have noted, their choice was in reality very restricted and Providence a risky light to follow. From the commencement of Lomé-1 to the mid-1980s French expenditure on aid to the Lomé partners grew as a proportion of total aid expenditure on them. British expenditure on aid to the same countries fell, as the Overseas Development Administration had wished. Two years after entry into the European Community the United Kingdom was the biggest exporter to the Lomé countries. Its share surpassed that of France by more than 10 per cent. By the period 1982–4 its share was much smaller than that of France (Table 3.1). British eyes remained fixed more on Asia. Britain's share of imports from the ACP countries also fell below that of France (Table 3.2).

Over all these negotiations the American demand for concessions still hovered, although the USA's case was a weaker one once it looked as though reverse preferences would not survive. The American Generalised Preference System made no progress in 1973 and was eventually withdrawn. Part of the background briefing for Edward Heath's meeting with President Nixon in January 1973 had been to remind the President that the UK had decided

Table 3.1 Trade effects of Lomé agreements 1975–84

	Pre-Lomé (%)	Lomé-1 1975–9 (%)	Lomé-2 1980–4 (%)
Share of EC-6 in commonwealth ACP exports	21.2	21.8	26.4
Share of EC-6 in non-oil commonwealth ACP exports	17.1	19.8	17.6
Share of UK in ACP exports	13.5	8.8	5.0
Share of UK in non-oil ACP exports	12.6	11.1	8.5
Share of UK in Yaoundé ACP exports	4.4	4.1	2.9

Table 3.2 Shares of EEC member-states in ACP exports to the Community (%)

	1970	1975	1979–81(av)	1982–4(av)
Belgium-Luxembourg	10.4	6.8	9.6	9.2
Denmark	0.7	1.4	1.2	0.9
France	19.6	24.4	25.5	27.2
Germany	13.3	14.7	23.1	22.4
Ireland	0.2	0.3	0.5	0.6
Italy	10.6	8.0	13.6	15.0
Netherlands	12.8	16.1	15.2	10.1
UK	34.2	28.3	11.2	13.9

that Treaties of Association for the Commonwealth ACP candidates were the desirable option and that therefore 'we should reiterate our view that it is wrong for the Americans to present the developing Commonwealth countries with the choice between association and participation in the US Generalised Preference Scheme'.[28] At the meeting, Heath insisted that the choice of association would 'help to maintain stability' both in Africa and the Caribbean, reminded him that when they had met in Bermuda in 1971 Nixon had expressed the wish that the UK should maintain an effective economic and political presence in the Caribbean, and that he hoped the issue would be dealt with on a case-by-case basis.[29] The USA was eventually to offer to withdraw its opposition in return for a share in the citrus fruit trade from the Mediterranean littoral to the EC, which suggests that the American policy had been from the beginning to use its opposition to the Lomé Convention as a bargaining counter for concessions in non-Lomé trade.

If eliminating reverse preferences was one of the aspects of Lomé-1 which made African countries hope that it would indeed be a new deal, it has to be written that the commodity composition of Africa's exports as well as their geographical distribution was hardly affected by the long wrangle and the change of rules it brought. Access to a wider market for the Commonwealth ACP states did not significantly affect their exports (Table 3.2). Before Lomé-1 their exports to the original six-member EEC averaged 21.2 per cent of their total exports by value. Under Lomé-1, from 1975 to 1979, the figure was 21.8 per cent. Under Lomé-2 (1980–4) it rose to 26.4 per cent. The rise however was due to increased oil exports from Nigeria. If oil exports are omitted from the calculation the share of exports going to the original six EC member-states was lower under Lomé-2 than Lomé-1. It fell from 19.8 per cent to 17.6 per cent. More striking, however, is the steep fall in the share of Commonwealth ACP states' exports to the United Kingdom. It fell from 8.8 per cent under Lomé-1 to 5 per cent under Lomé-2. The share of the United Kingdom in the exports of the former Yaoundé Convention members fell similarly.

As for British exports to the ACP countries, the steep decline in their share of total ACP imports under the first Lomé Convention was statistically comparable to the steep increase of that of France (Table 3.3). Confining the picture to the European Community and the ACP countries, it would seem as though eliminating 'reciprocity' was a point of principle for the future, making little practical difference at the time. However, widening the picture to include the rest of the world puts a somewhat different gloss on the picture. While eliminating reverse preferences did not significantly reduce the dependence of the francophone states on the French market, the more developed British West African states increased their exports to non-European markets, particularly the USA. Had the USA's protests been intended to impose restrictions on imports from countries which had signed the original French proposals for Lomé, it would have been Ghana and Nigeria which would have been most in danger.

Freed from reverse preferences and from the possibility of American restrictions on them because of their preferences on European markets, the

Table 3.3 Shares of EEC member-states in ACP imports from the Community (%)

	1970	1975	1979–81(av)	1982–4(av)
Belgium-Luxembourg	6.7	5.8	6.0	6.1
Denmark	1.3	1.4	1.4	1.9
France	25.1	27.8	31.5	34.8
Germany	15.8	18.9	17.7	15.3
Ireland	0.3	0.3	0.6	0.7
Italy	8.5	9.1	10.2	12.7
Netherlands	7.0	6.7	8.0	7.5
UK	35.5	30.3	24.7	21.0

African Lomé states nevertheless lost ground in world trade and became, as noted, increasingly marginalised. What part did Europe, the main destination of Africa's exports, play in this marginalisation?

The Franco–British dispute over the relationship of the Lomé Conventions to the increasing liberalisation and globalisation of international trade should be seen more as an anxious prelude to what might happen than as a struggle between protectionists and liberalisers. There was such a struggle both in London and Paris, but the more salient argument between the two countries was over the extent to which African economies could respond to globalised trading rules and the extent to which they needed special provision.

The source of the persistent pressures to liberalise world trade since the Second World War is a disputed matter. It is attributed to the behaviour of firms, to that of domestic political institutions, to particular characteristics of national governments and to the nature of the post-war international relations system. The behaviour of firms can be seen as a reaction to the abundance and cost of the factors of production, as it was in the earliest Ricardian models seeking to explain the very existence of international trade. Firms depending on relatively abundant factors will advocate free trade; firms dependent on scarcer factors are more likely to seek more protectionist arrangements. They are moved to action by changes in their income.

Since, however, after 1945 government was visibly and audibly in charge of trade policy in the years we are considering, it is not reasonable to rely solely on any explanation depending on the behaviour of firms without linking it in some way to governments or other institutions. Some electoral systems are, it can be argued, less amenable to protectionist lobby groups than others and such systems, it can also be argued, were more strongly established in Europe than elsewhere, whence the extent of tariff reductions and removals in post-1945 Europe. To many experts in international relations, however, liberalisation and globalisation are attributed primarily to the domination of the international system by an extremely powerful hegemon, the USA.

None of these explanations carries much conviction for a historian. When much trade in manufactures in the 1950s, particularly within western Europe, consisted of ships and trains passing in opposite directions loaded with products almost indistinguishable except by brand name from each other, it is difficult to see how factors of production could have much to do with such a process. National governments moved towards increasing liberalisation in the 1950s because foreign trade became so important a source of wealth and income. It sustained the long post-war boom and as it did so the arguments for protectionism particularly in western Europe lost most of their force. The characteristic of western European government in that period was the uninterrupted increases in its spending capability which continually expanding foreign trade and high rates of GNP growth allowed. As for the role of the hegemon, its own political system was notoriously open to protectionist lobby groups.

One aspect of any explanation is, however, clear. Only states could liberalise and only states could establish and uphold the convertibility of their currencies. International institutions – GATT, the World Bank, the International Monetary Fund – existed to control a liberalisation initiated by states. In such a system African states were in a weak position. In international organisations they were more beggars than policy initiators. The intra-trade which was so powerful a force for growth, and thus for further liberalisation, within western Europe, had no counterpart within the African continent. The tendency of African governments was to protect what they had, lest they should end up with even less. The sources of increasing wealth in Europe or America were intermittent trickles in Africa. The Lomé Conventions discouraged their flow as much as or more than they stimulated them. The Lomé countries were outside the power structure in Brussels, but could not abandon the links with Europe, because it remained their best market.

In such a situation participation in a widespread, multilateral, non-discriminatory trading system would only emphasise their political weakness within the system. There are several probable reasons why a discriminatory, preferential system might have been seen as more satisfactory, although proving this to have been so would be very difficult. A study of the French government's aid packages to Africa under François Mitterand's presidency might reveal that a bigger element of preferential protectionism brought with it a greater concentration of aid on selected tasks. This, though, would fall well short of the agenda of the less developed countries in the post-Lomé trading framework. That agenda includes the liberalisation of agricultural markets as well as textile markets; freedom from United States' anti-dumping legislation; the import of generic medicines at lower prices than those asked by major pharmaceutical multinationals, technical aid to argue their corner in international trade regulatory institutions and so on. These disputes were all present in Lomé's last decade. The agenda has grown with the problems, the solutions have not.

It is in this worldwide context that the erosion of the Yaoundé and Lomé preferences has to be seen. It was the outcome of the reduction of British tariffs in adaptation to the Common External Tariff and of the progressive reduction through tariff bargaining of the Common External Tariff itself. Any attempt by France to protect its African territories was bound to bring a clash between France's role as a world trader and its tutelary role in francophone Africa, a clash in which its interests as a world trader were bound ultimately to triumph. The erosion of the preferences applied to all ACP states; British policy was on the same rack as that of France and it would make the same choice. The inexorability of this process was underlined by the undertaking by the European Community at the United Nations Conference on Trade and Development (UNCTAD) meeting in 1968 to set up a worldwide UN Generalised System of Preferences. That system was already in operation in 1971, two years after the EEC's trade agreements with Tunisia and Morocco offered both countries preferential access to its markets on terms for certain goods more generous than those of Yaoundé-2. The majority of ACP export product groups by the 1980s were imported on the same terms into the European Union as products from other under-developed lands, through zero-rated, most-favoured-nation (MFN) tariffs, as laid down in the Lomé Conventions, or through zero-rated tariffs fixed by the EU's own Generalised System of Preferences. About 8 per cent only of the exports of ACP countries to the EU in the 1980s had a preferential tariff differential greater than 5 per cent.[30]

Attempts to measure the precise impact of that surviving differential are beset by many problems of measurement. Sapir's study of the years 1967–78 concluded that the dummy variables that he used to reflect the EEC Generalised System of Preferences status of an exporting country in bilateral trade were statistically significant only for 1973 and 1974.[31] Those were two of Lomé's best years. If the categories of goods taken into account were reduced to machinery and manufactures (SITC 7 and 8) the statistical significance of generalised preferences was somewhat greater. In those two SITC categories African exports to the EC were, of course, negligible quantities. This does not mean that generalised preferences necessarily made competition by African exports much harder, especially as it must be assumed that over that period a high proportion continued to be 'tied' exports. A study by Langhammer for the years 1978–80 suggests, on the evidence of this very short period, that exports to the Community from developed countries grew faster than those from beneficiary countries of the Generalised Preference Scheme.[32] Since African developing countries, however, had a much more limited range of exports to offer, the plausible conclusion we might draw is that the elimination of their preference margins by worldwide preference schemes made little difference to their situation.

The longer term aim of the African states in Lomé had to be structural diversification of their exports in the direction of semi-manufactures and manufactures. It was there that the 'rules of origin' written into the Lomé Conventions struck hard. African states setting foot on the first rungs of the typical ladder of industrialisation produced wood products, textiles, clothing and leather goods, much as European states had done in climbing the same ladder in the seventeenth and eighteenth centuries when they had sold similar products to West Africa among their many other markets. Harder times in Europe after 1973 were, however, quickly attributed, without much evidence, to competition in manufactures with less developed countries. While competition there was indeed from the so-called 'next developing countries', competition from the less developed countries was insignificant. Where such competition could be located, it was surely a message for change in Europe rather than preservation of industrial enterprises with no outlook other than permanent protection.

Nevertheless, protection against textile imports by the whole of the developed world was the purpose of the Multifibre Arrangement, which imposed quotas on yarn, textiles and clothing imports from less developed countries into western Europe and the USA and the Lomé Conventions provided no exemption. The rules of origin, in fact, made it more difficult. Clothing and textiles to qualify for a preference under Lomé, before in many cases meeting a quota restriction, had to be manufactured from non-imported yarn. Throughout the whole range of industrial processing similar restrictions applied. Canned fish fell foul of the rules of origin if the can was not made in the country whose fishermen caught the fish, a regulation which prevented even the export of tinned sardines.

Such rules denied the advantage of trans-border interchange in manufacturing. By contrast, EEC countries were allowed to set up simple assembly industries in the ACP countries. The official Community defence of these policies was that the rules deterred footloose foreign direct investment, which indicates some measure of difference between the attitudes of the EEC to underdeveloped Ireland and to its truly poor Lomé 'partners'. French and British processing firms, of course, were unlikely to be footloose when they were engaged in processing a captive source of raw material before transhipping it to the metropole.

It followed that processing in the African states was for the most part at an unsophisticated level. In descending order of value the manufactured exports of the ACP countries to the EU in 1992 were boats, cotton fabrics, leather, processed wood, knitwear and clocks. Other categories were of insignificant value. Boats were a Caribbean export. Of the other, African, products, the main exporters were Ivory Coast, Ghana and Cameroon, areas where European traders had first traded extensively with Africa. From cocoa and slaves to cotton cloth and clocks in three centuries was not a rapid advance. Away from the western coast of Africa the advance was slower.

In using rules of origin to protect jobs and output in its own territory the EU was hampering both the structural and the geographical diversification of African exports. If one fundamental problem for the African states was that they had little to export, when they did find something Europe would not buy it. In an African world where only Ghana, Ivory Coast, Madagascar, Nigeria and Sénégal had significant exports outside the European Community only a relaxation of Community rules could change the situation.

The non-tariff barriers which made it difficult for African states to develop processing industries were the harder to surmount because of the inconsistency and short duration of single aid projects. The clash of concepts and ideologies of trade within the EC was affected by shifts in the concept of economic development which were common throughout the developed world. The varying theoretical categorisations of the historical process of economic development closely affected arguments about the relationship of aid to development.

For a further decade after the end of the great European boom in 1973 thinking about economic development referred always to the power of foreign trade to create growth, as it had done in the boom. The prevailing criticisms of the Lomé Conventions remained, therefore, that they did not provide the underdeveloped African states with enough possibility of increased earnings in foreign markets, whether in Europe or Africa. Commercial enterprise, however, was thought, or deduced from historical experience, to respond to every possibility of gain, changing the nature of the underdeveloped society as it did so. Although Europe was to blame for protecting substantial sectors of its economy against the exports of the poor, access to markets on a large enough scale would nevertheless increase Africa's exports and its GNP.

In the 1980s, however, political science introduced a much more complex proposition: although it was true that European states were selfishly and wrongly protecting jobs in industries which it would have been wiser to replace by higher technologies, this did not mean that Europe was responsible for the poor performance of African economies. Those economies were, after all, getting international help on a co-ordinated scale in a way that had not previously happened in history. The blame for the disappointments of Lomé should, therefore, be at least shared by African states which had proved incapable of taking advantage of what they had been offered. Administrative incompetence, inability to agree amongst themselves, corruption and, above all, lack of properly functioning democratic government were to blame. In this view can be seen the line of thought which has now in the early twenty-first century had a resurgence in categorising some states as 'failed states' and correlating their failures with their unwillingness to copy in detail the political processes of the USA or the European Community states. It was political, not economic, processes which, it was alleged, rendered Lomé so ineffective. Above all, the African states, it was argued, lacked in comparison to their European partners the sense of a common national identity and purpose which, so political scientists and some historians asserted, was the prime impulse for economic growth. This was uneasy territory for an international organisation which insisted on its own 'supranationality' as a signpost for the rest of the world.

Fashion changed again in the 1990s when anthropology made serious inroads into development economics. In anthropological perspective, the Lomé Conventions were far away from feeding the true roots of economic development. Development was, indeed, anthropologists argued, driven by markets, but within local, not national, communities. Within communities social and economic particularities determined the degree of responsiveness to markets and economic opportunity. This was supported by a rapidly increasing volume of historical writing about the true origins of industrial-isation in European states and in the USA, demonstrating that the first steps in development, while they certainly had much to do with the availability of other places in the world as markets, were dependent on local cultural dynamics and indeed resembled rather closely a pattern of first steps which were theoretically possible in poor, culturally divided, and fundamentally local African states. The implication was that it was illogical to try to feed the local roots of economic advance by large but haphazard trade and aid programmes drafted on a national or supranational level between govern-ments and which resulted in single huge development projects. These were more likely to drown local communities than to set them on a voyage to prosperity. Lomé stood, before the present decade, at the bar of history, accused of confounding economic rationality with the rationalisations of a post-Industrial Revolution mercantile society which had created its own simplified image of how it had become rich, simplifying in the process the variety of local market relationships out of which economic advance had in reality flowered.[33] It might be remarked that if that were so anthropology had done something to produce that result because of the centrality of markets to its thinking. Yet it was true that many of the larger projects financed by Lomé were hugely inappropriate to the task on hand.

Does the fact that the economic behaviour of the British and French states conformed to these international trends, therefore not explain much about the real significance of the Franco–British agreement on the Lomé Conv-entions? Once the ungenerous deployment of non-tariff barriers by the European Community against the exports of its poorest associates, together with the erosion of their privileges by generalised preference schemes, is taken into full consideration with the steady determination of the United Kingdom not to allow the provision of aid to Africa to exceed the low ceiling that it was so intent on preserving to make way for aid to Asian exporters, it seems clear that Lomé was not actually intended as a new deal. That the United Kingdom and France each having granted independence to a large empire in Africa had a common interest in working together there is true, but it did not stop opposed points of view from being so strongly upheld that it was as difficult to come to terms about a cooperative framework for trade as it was for aid. Once they did achieve a common policy administered by the European Community it covered only a small part of their aid to Africa, while they appear to have had no programme at all of common political action there.

Were the Lomé Conventions then mere symbolism to emphasise that two imperialist countries had submerged their international rivalry into a permanently peaceful Europe? Had it been so, the struggle to agree would not have been so hard fought. Had they been intended to have changed the political scheme of things in Africa, they would have been much harder fought.

The accession of the UK to the European Community brought two important changes to Directorate-General 8 of the European Commission, the DG responsible for development. They provide a partial answer. The initial domination of DG-8 by French officials, and the role of Jacques Ferrandi, could not have survived the expansion of the Community, not least because of the disillusionment of some of his French colleagues with his personalised working methods of disbursing and directing aid to those states and statesmen with which he had particularly strong connections. It was in fact a one-man show, about which British officials also complained vigorously. It was important to them that Ferrandi should go if there was to be a more rational, more bureaucratic and less 'colonialist' procedure in Brussels. Already in the 1930s and more strongly after 1945 French officials had sought, like their British counterparts, to establish a less colonialist and more national form of imperial administration and there had been discussions between the two countries about this.[34] When Cheysson became Director-General he was supportive of more rational and methodical methods of aid allocation and programming. Economists replaced mysterious 'contacts' and personal decision-making. This change in working procedures itself argued for a change from Yaoundé to Lomé and for the admission of the Caribbean and Pacific states to Lomé. The Lomé regime in its turn stimulated a more bureaucratic rationale in aid allocation. A former British politician, Maurice Foley, became the deputy head of DG-8 as Cheysson's choice. British belief that closer cooperation in Africa would be possible rose noticeably when Ferrandi left. The mere fact of Community expansion by itself, it could be argued, brought a current of administrative change which made Anglo–French economic cooperation in Africa more feasible. If it was not undertaken more boldly, this might be blamed on the financial restrictions which Britain maintained on aid. But in view of France's ready acceptance of the low level of the European Development Fund and the much greater size of bilateral aid, such reasoning would not match the evidence.

A somewhat more convincing explanation can be found in delegation theory. It was important to France that the existing European Community programme of aid to Africa be maintained. If it were to lapse because of

Community expansion, the longer term financing of the Community's 'own resources' might continue to be called into question. If it were upheld, the British contribution to the European Development Fund would be as big as that of France and the continuity of finance for the development of its former empire, which France had demanded but failed to win in the negotiations for the Treaty of Rome, would be secured. There were therefore real and immediate gains to be made by France in establishing a joint programme with Britain for the ACP countries. Britain's gain was in establishing its willingness to work within the administrative framework of the Community to advance a core Community project. It was a credible commitment to the future purpose of the European Community, when full acceptance of the CAP and the CFP after entry were not. Such an outcome would be predicted by the theory of delegation. Both countries delegated a sum of money, small in comparison with their future national expenditures on bilateral aid, to DG-8 and the European Commission to spend as part of a Community-wide project as a pledge of credibility and in France's case to to secure permanent 'own resources' for the Community.

The first expansion of the European Community, if considered as a merely European event, could be interpreted as giving some support to what were at the time the more fashionable theories about its inherent tendency to grow. That its bounds in Europe would be set wider still and wider, because functionalist politics was the appropriate and rational response to the political and economic pressure on Europe, appeared to be substantiated by the first expansion, and particularly by the overthrow through political and economic pressures from within and without of France's policy of keeping the United Kingdom out.[35] With that change of policy the Lomé Conventions marked an assertion that Europe would continue to play a major role in Africa. The failure of France's attempts to create a political union, at first of its colonies and then of independent francophone states, in Africa, made Lomé an even stronger avowal of the need for common European action. The first African state in the post-war world to receive independence from the United Kingdom was Ghana, whose leader, Kwame Nkrumah, was a fervent advocate of an African political union. What came instead, in both anglophone and francophone black Africa, was a competing world of weak nation-states striving, fairly unsuccessfully, to replicate that pattern in Europe whose replacement by a more appropriate political system was trumpeted in speeches about the European Community's ability to include its two most powerful nation-states in a common framework for political action.

It seems absurd to argue that the Lomé Conventions sprang therefore out of any functionalist political process of solving problems in common. What France and the United Kingdom agreed was to pursue their own separate national policies in Africa and to legitimate their decision by also constituting a common EU trade framework for EU–African trade, linked to a common, but small, EU aid programme backed by a European Development Fund (EDF). A more plausible theoretical explanation lies in the delegation theory fashionable in institutional history to explain why national governments increasingly delegate tasks to separate agencies. The relationships between principals (national governments) and their agents are contractual ones. The most-studied examples, those from which the theory is mainly derived, are between the Congress of the United States and the various agents to which it delegates the implementation and oversight of particular legislation or even of some everyday responsibilities of government.

The rationale for such delegation rests on the theory that it reduces transaction costs for governments. After considering the serious differences of opinion cited earlier between the United Kingdom and France the reader might be willing to categorise these as high transaction costs which would have been always recurring had it not been possible to transfer the administration of their common objective to the European Commission. One outcome of this, was, of course, that it would be very difficult to change the rules of Lomé-1, because to do so would reopen high-cost political trans-actions and disputes. The administrative changes in DG-8 were an example of such high transaction costs which not all of the French administrative machine thought it desirable to pay.

For the United Kingdom, Lomé-1 was important as a pledge of credibility to the European Community of the kind that the French government wanted to see and which the United Kingdom wanted to give in order to emphasise its commitment to the Community. Pledges of credibility are frequently observed to be made by principals when a similar process of delegation takes place at the level of national government. To make such a pledge of credibility to a supranational government was a much larger gesture by two such powerful states as Britain and France. Africa thenceforward had a third interlocutor with which it could also negotiate issues of trade and aid, the EC. The act of delegation was also a pledge of credibility and continuity to Africa.

There is, though, a further assertion frequently made about delegation theory, that it leads to more efficient decision-making. The agent is not distracted by febrile daily thoughts about the links between policy and votes and is allegedly freer from the lobbying of interest-groups than national government.

Quite irrespective of whether this is generally true of the United States, Britain or France, it is not a useful argument to explain Lomé. The ultimate decision-making power did not lie with the European Commission but with the Council of Ministers, the representatives of national government. The delegation of a common programme for Africa to the European

Commission was in reality a contract open to intervention from the national governments of nine countries. The Congress of the USA is a parliament, but for most of the period covered by the Lomé Conventions the European Parliament could be left off the organigram. The agent was always and immediately responsible to the wills of an increasing number of national governments whose wishes could change, or prevent change in, the implicit contract. It is unlikely that greater efficiency of decision-making would ensue from any act of delegation in which six or more governments are constantly involved in ensuring, or failing to ensure, the 'right' decision. It is only fair to remember, at this point, that the decisions in question were foreign policy decisions and that the delegation of foreign policy by national states to agencies has not been so noticeable either in the USA or in the European Union.

Much of the theoretical discussion about principals and agents turns on the question of the control of the agent. Does the agent have its own policy preferences and does it advance them? Does it have its own, separate agenda? Does it make its own regulatory rules? Does it enforce them? The more the answers to these questions are positive, the more it can be argued that it is through the agencies of the European Union that functionalist political theory has been reinstated as a force for political integration.

Directorate-General 8 of the European Commission did have its own agenda. Once Claude Cheysson was in charge of it, Maurice Foley, whom he brought in as Deputy Director-General, pushed for a more energetic policy-making role for the Community. In the negotiations for Lomé-1 the Commission was a strong advocate of a single uniform design for the Treaties of Association, even when the British government had not yet reached any final decision about reverse preferences. In the absence of any significant case being brought before the European Court of Justice, it is not really possible to reach a verdict about the Commission's enforcement activities. The agenda of the Commission as a whole was to expand Europe's interest in Africa. The expansion of the preferential trade treaties is in itself evidence of the European Community's own policy preferences.

The Lomé Conventions were international treaties, not amendable by the European Parliament. Attempts at regulating the European Development Fund by national parliaments would make little impression on the Conventions, because delegating the fund's implementation made it difficult to bring pressure to bear on its operational rules. The transaction costs would have been higher for reformers reforming the Lomé programme than for reforming national aid policy and, because the Lomé programme was smaller than national programmes of bilateral aid, there would have been a smaller gain in return for that higher cost. That conclusion assumes that reform would have been possible, which is far from certain.

The Franco–British agreement on which the Lomé Conventions rested, does not seem to have been designed for change. The trade rules were those of already existing international bodies. It was designed as a political fixture, leaving ample room for separate national policies, provided the commitment to the EU was maintained. The responsibility of agents has already invoked a substantial literature on the way parliaments control their performance, but parliaments and governments can delegate as a way of avoiding final responsibility. Changes in the rules of Lomé of the specific nature that the African states asked for would have opened the door to similar concessions in the national bilateral aid programmes where national governments would not have made the EU's interventions welcome. This would have involved the EU in trying to push the changes through international agencies and meetings where Africa's requests would have been micro-business compared to the much greater issues on the agenda. It would have also required reaching agreement with France and the UK and then winning the agreement of the other member-states. All this was beyond the EU's range. The outcome was that the Lomé Conventions were a delegation to limbo, designed more to shelve a problem than to solve it.

The blame for this does not fall on the European Commission, something better for the ACP states was on its agenda. In questions of the relation of national expenditures to foreign policy it was never to become even an agent. Given the great scope of its powers in the regulation of international commerce, neither France nor Britain was ever likely to propose giving the Commission similar powers to bargain with Africa and to adapt and rewrite treaties which for them were a small but satisfactory working arrangement, leaving them plenty of scope for their own individual devices. Europe could fly its flag where the Union Jack and the Tricolore had once prevailed. The European Community expansion could, commercially, cover a vast non-European territory. If things went wrong, supranational Europe would have to share the blame. There seems very little political theory about delegation as a way of stopping things being done. The Lomé Conventions, with their diffused responsibilities, might be a good place to start. In that respect they seem to have faithfully followed the habit of Empire.

Notes

1 Economics and politics in the decision to join the European Union

1 Eurostat, *External and Intra-European Trade. Statistical Yearbook. Data 1958–2001* (Brussels: Eurostat, 2002).
2 U. Moorthy, 'Attitudes to the European Project – the Eurobarometer Perspective', Paper presented to the Einstein Forum, 'Realizing Europe', Potsdam, 24–25 January 2003.
3 J. Viner, *The Customs Union Issue* (New York: Carnegie Endowment for International Peace, 1950).
4 J. Gillingham, *European Integration, 1950–2003. Superstate or New Market Economy?* (Cambridge: Cambridge University Press, 2003).
5 B. Eichengreen, J. Frieden and J. von Hagen (eds), *Monetary and Fiscal Policy in an Integrated Europe* (Berlin and Heidelberg, Springer Verlag, 1995).
6 All calculations derived from European Free Trade Association, *EFTA Trade 1959–1967* (Geneva: EFTA, 1969), pp. 72–3.
7 Ibid., p. 73.
8 European Free Trade Association, *The Trade Effects of EFTA and the EEC 1959–1967* (Geneva: EFTA, 1972), pp. 94–102; 110–19.
9 P. Lains, *Os Progressos do Atraso, Uma Nova História Económica de Portugal* (Lisbon: Imprensa de Ciências Sociais, 2003), p. 184.
10 J.E. Meade, *The Theory of Customs Unions* (Amsterdam: North Holland, 1955).
11 R.G. Lipsey, *Theory of Customs Unions: A General Equilibrium Analysis* (London: Weidenfeld & Nicolson, 1970).
12 A.S. Milward, *The European Rescue of the Nation-State* (2nd edn, London: Routledge, 1994), pp. 134–67.
13 T. Tewes, 'Handelschaffende und handelumlenkende Wirkungen der EWG bei der deutschen Einfuhr unter besonderer Berücksichtigung der EFTA-Länder', *Weltwirtschaftliches Archiv*, 106 (1971), pp. 221–39.
14 T. Scitovsky, *Economic Theory and European Integration* (London: Allen & Unwin, 1958).
15 As they are at times in Gillingham, *European Integration*.
16 R.E. Baldwin, 'A domino theory of regionalism', in R.E. Baldwin, P. Haaparanta and J. Kiander (eds) *Expanding Membership of the European Union* (Cambridge: Cambridge University Press, 1995).

118   *Notes*

T. Rhenisch, *Europäische Integration und industrielles Interesse: Die Deutsche Industrie und die Gründung der europäischen Wirtschaftsgemeinschaft* (Stuttgart: Steiner Verlag, 1999).
18 M. Schulte, 'Challenging the Common Market project: German industry, Britain and Europe, 1957–63', in A. Deighton and A.S. Milward (eds) *Widening, Deepening and Acceleration 1957–1963* (Baden-Baden: Nomos Verlag, 1999).
19 B. de Witte, 'The past and future role of the European Court of Justice in the protection of human rights', in P. Alston, M. Bustelo and J. Heenan (eds) *The EU and Human Rights* (Oxford: Clarendon Press, 1999).
20 See the fuller discussion by M. Newman, 'The European Union and Human Rights', in E.A. Koladziej (ed.) *A Force Profonde: The Power, Politics and Promise of Human Rights* (Philadelphia, PA: University of Pennsylvania Press, 2003).
21 M. af Malmborg, *Den Ståndaktiga Nationalstaten. Sverige och den Västeeuropeiska Integrationen 1945–1959* (Bibliotheca Historica Lundensis 80, Lund: Lund University Press, 1994), pp. 49–59.
22 Idem, 'Sweden's long road to an agreement with the EEC 1956–1972', in M. Gehler and R. Steininger (eds) *Die Neutrale und die europäische Integration 1945–1995* (Vienna: Böhlau Verlag, 2000), p. 309–36.
23 M. Gehler, 'Zwischen Supranationalität und Gaullismus. Österreich und die europäische Integration 1957–1963', pp. 309–36, and R. Steininger, 'Österreichs "Alleingang" nach Brüssel 1963–1969', pp. 577–644; ibid., pp. 497–576.
24 F.R. Willis, *France, Germany and the New Europe 1945–67* (Stanford: Stanford University Press, 1968); J. Gillingham, *Coal, Steel and the Rebirth of Europe, 1945–1955. The Germans and French from Ruhr Conflict to Economic Community* (Cambridge: Cambridge University Press, 1991); I. Warner, *Steel and Sovereignty. The Deconcentration of the West German Steel Industry, 1949–1954*, (Mainz: P. von Zabern, 1996); T. Witschke, *Gefahr für den Wettbewerb? Die Fusionskontrolle der Europäischen Gemeinschaft für Kohle und Stahl (EGKS) und die 'Rekonzentration' der Ruhrstahlindustrie 1950–1963* (PhD thesis, European University Institute, 2003).
25 E.B. Haas, *The Uniting of Europe. Political, Social and Economic Forces, 1950–1957* (Stanford: Stanford University Press, 1958); idem, *Beyond the Nation State: Functionalism and International Organization* (Stanford: Stanford University Press, 1964); L.N. Lindberg, *The Political Dynamics of European Economic Integration* (Stanford: Stanford University Press, 1963). E.B. Haas, *The Uniting of Europe*, 2nd edn (1968), took a much more cautious view of his earlier argument.
26 D. Mitrany, 'The prospect of integration: federal or functional', in A.J.R. Groom and P. Taylor (eds), *Functionalism: Theory and Practice in International Relations* (New York: Crane, Russak, 1975).
27 A.S. Milward, F.M.B. Lynch, F. Romero, R. Ranieri and V. Sørensen, *The Frontier of National Sovereignty. History and Theory 1945–1992* (London: Routledge, 1993).
28 A.S. Milward, *European Rescue*.
29 K.W. Deutsch, S.A. Burrel, R.A. Kann, M. Lee, Jnr, M. Lighterman, R.E. Lindgren, F.L. Loewenheim and R.W. van Wagenen, *Political Community and the North Atlantic Area: International Organization in the Light of Historical Experience* (Princeton: Princeton University Press, 1957).

30 A. Moravcsik, 'Preferences and power in the European Community: a liberal intergovernmentalist approach', *Journal of Common Market Studies*, 31(4) (1993) pp. 473–524; ibid., *The Choice for Europe: Social Purpose and State Power from Messina to Maastricht* (Ithaca, NY: Cornell University Press, 1998)

31 W. Wessels, 'An ever closer fusion: a dynamic macropolitical view on integration processes', *Journal of Common Market Studies*, 35(2) (1997), pp. 267–99.

2 Denmark, Ireland and the political economy of industrialisation

1 Calculations made from national accounts by A. Boltho, *The European Economy: Growth and Crisis* (Oxford: Oxford University Press, 1982), p. 34. Real GDP grew over the period 1960–8 in Denmark at an average of 4.6 per cent, in Norway at 4.4 per cent, in Ireland at 4.2 per cent and in the UK at 3.0 per cent, when the average for OECD European countries was 4.7 per cent. (OECD, *Historical Statistics*, Paris: OECD, 1991), p. 48.

2 H.C. Johansen, *Dansk Historisk Statistik 1814–1980* (Copenhagen: Gyldendal, 1985), pp. 208–11 (tables 4.5a, 4.5b); *Historisk Statistikk, 1978* (Oslo: Statistisk Sentralbyrå, 1978).

3 Danish Ministry of Foreign Affairs, *Economic Survey of Denmark 1961* (Copenhagen: J.H. Schultz Forlag, 1961).

4 E. O'Malley, *Industry and Economic Development: The Challenge for the Latecomer* (Dublin: Gill & Macmillan, 1989) is a wide-ranging and penetrative study of Ireland's industrialisation in its international setting. The domestic politics of industrialisation are discussed in J.J. Lee, *Ireland, 1912–1985: Politics and Society* (Cambridge: Cambridge University Press, 1989). The effect of industrialisation on Irish commercial diplomacy is methodically traced in D.J. Maher, *The Tortuous Path: The Course of Ireland's Entry into the EEC, 1948–73* (Dublin: Institute of Public Administration, 1986). The immediate road to the Anglo-Irish Free Trade Agreement is more fully discussed in M. Fitzgerald, *Protectionism to Liberalisation: Ireland and the EEC, 1957 to 1966* (Aldershot: Ashgate, 2000).

5 Estimates of labour-force distribution and composition of national product from, respectively, OECD, Department of Economics and Statistics, *Labour Force Statistics* (1966–88) and B.R. Mitchell, *European Historical Statistics 1750–1970* (1978 edn), pp. 427, 429 (New York: Columbia University Press, 1978). National Income from OECD, *National Accounts of OECD Countries, 1950–1978*, vol. 1 (Paris: OECD, 1980).

6 E.F. Nash and E.A. Attwood, *The Agricultural Policies of Britain and Denmark. A Study in Reciprocal Trade* (London: Land Books Ltd, 1961).

7 A. Ølgaard, *The Danish Economy* (Commission of the European Communities Collection Studies, Economic and Financial Series, 14, Brussels: CEC, 1980), p. 178.

8 A. Maizels, *Industrial Growth and World Trade* (Cambridge: Cambridge University Press, 1963).

9 L. Mjøset, *The Irish Economy in a Comparative Institutional Perspective* (Dublin: National Economic and Social Council, 1992).

10 A. Lehmann, 'Venstres vej til Europa: Venstres europapolitik 1945–1960', *Den Jyske Historiker*, 93 (September 2001), pp. 32–52.

11   Maher, *Tortuous Path*, p. 58.

12   Cited ibid., p. 55.

13   Ibid., p. 56.

14   Ibid., p. 67.

15   Ibid., p. 56. The Department might have added the right of Irish citizens resident in Britain to vote in British elections, a 'European right' which the European Union still seems scarcely able to contemplate. The comparison with Benelux was ambivalent, for Benelux before the Treaty of Rome was no more than a very incomplete common market, showing few signs of progressing further.

16   Ibid., p. 68. The link between free trade and nineteenth-century 'colonialism' became a gospel of Irish nationalism. Had there truly been a rigid application of free trade in the nineteenth century there would have been no tariffs on grain to repeal at the time of the famine and Ireland's most terrible memory might have been less terrible.

17   Fitzgerald, *Protectionism*, gives the fullest account, emphasising the importance of prospective accession to the EU.

18   V. Sørensen, *Denmark's Social Democratic Government and the Marshall Plan 1947–1950* (Copenhagen: Museum Tusculanum Press, 2001).

19   V. Sørensen, 'Between interdependence and integration: Denmark's shifting strategies', in A.S. Milward, F.M.B. Lynch, F. Romero, R. Ranieri and V. Sørensen (eds), op. cit., pp. 88–116.

20   J.N. Laursen and T.B. Olesen, 'A Nordic alternative to Europe? The interdependence of Denmark's Nordic and European policies, 1945–1998', *Contemporary European History*, 1 (2000), pp. 120–39, provide a political and economic overview of the questions raised by these intra-Scandinavian negotiations. The more precise economic issues of the 1960s are discussed in T.B. Olesen and J.N. Laursen, 'Danmarks lange vej til EF-medlemskab, 1960–72', in T. Swienty (ed.) *Danmark i Europa 1945–1993* (Copenhagen: Munksgaard, 1994), pp. 131–55.

21   V. Sørensen, 'Nordic cooperation: a social democratic alternative to Europe?' in T.B. Olesen, *Interdependence versus Integration: Denmark, Scandinavia and Western Europe 1945–1960* (Odense: Odense University Press, 1995), pp. 40–61.

22   D. Larsen, *Et Land i Europa. Venstre i 125 År* (Copenhagen: Venstres Pressetjeneste, 1995), pp. 170–3.

23   M. Rasmussen, 'Ivar Nørgaards mareridt: Socialdemokratiet og den Økonomiske og Monetære Union 1970–1972', *Den Jyske Historiker*, 93 (2001), pp. 73–95.

24   J.O. Krag, *Le Danemark à l'heure du Marché Commun* (Paris: Plon, 1974), entry for 1 February 1972.

25   H. Allen, *Norway and Europe in the 1970s*, (Oslo: Universitetsforlaget, 1979), p. 150. The slogan was coined by Arne Kielland, author, also, of one of the many conflicting and *parti-pris* analyses of the reason for the government's defeat in the referendum; A. Kielland, 'Skillelinjer i norsk politikk', *Samtiden*, 6 (1971), pp. 348–59.

26   For an analysis of the cleavages in Norwegian politics which led to the rejection of Community membership in terms of the 'political economy' of Norway, H.-O. Frøland, 'Choosing the periphery: the political economy of Norway's European integration policy, 1948–1973', *Journal of European Integration History*, 7(1) (2001), pp. 77–103.

27 N. Petersen, 'Holdninger til europæisk integration og EF-folkeafstemningen 1972', *Økonomi og Politik*, 50 (1976), pp. 24–51. 'Attitudes towards European integration and the Danish common market referendum', *Scandinavian Political Studies*, 1(1) (1978), pp. 2–27.
28 E. O'Malley, *Industry*, p. 101, table 6.2.
29 Ibid., p. 104, table 6.4.
30 R. O'Donnell, 'The internal market', in P. Keatinge (ed.) *Ireland and EC Membership Evaluated* (London: Pinter Publishers, 1991), p. 31. For more detail on geographical distribution and on rates of export growth net of market growth, D. McAleese, 'Ireland and the European Community: the changing pattern of trade', in P.J. Drudy and D. McAleese (eds) *Ireland and the European Community* (Cambridge: Cambridge University Press, 1984).
31 E. O'Malley, *Industry*, p. 89.
32 R. O'Donnell, 'The internal market', op. cit.
33 G. Fitzgerald, 'Ireland and the European challenge', in D. Keogh (ed.) *Ireland and the Challenge of European Integration* (Cork: Hibernian University Press, 1989).
34 OECD, *Historical Statistics, 1960–1989*, table 3.1 (Paris: OECD, 1991).

3 Europe's Africa

1 H. d'Almeida Topor and M. Lakroum, *L'Europe et l'Afrique. Un siècle d'échanges économiques* (Paris: Armand Colin, 1994), pp. 60–5.
2 Article 131 of the Treaty establishing the European Economic Community.
3 NA, PREM 15/365. Record of the Prime Minister's meeting with Mr Mitchell Sharp, Canadian Secretary of State for External Affairs, on 26 November 1970.
4 Ibid., FCO telegram to Washington Embassy, 1 January 1971, 'The United States and Commonwealth Association with the EEC'.
5 Ibid.
6 NA, PREM 15/364. *Note for the Record*. Prime Minister's entertainment of M. Jean-François Deniau to dinner at Chequers, 3 January 1971.
7 I. Begg, F. Cripps and T. Ward, 'The European Community: problems and prospects', *Cambridge Economic Policy Review*, 7(2) (December 1981), p. 28, table 3.4.
8 J. Moss and J. Ravenhill, 'Trade between the ACP and EEC during Lomé-1', in C. Stevens (ed.) *EEC and the Third World: A Survey 3* (London: Hodder & Stoughton, 1983), p. 140.
9 NA, Cabinet Office, GEN131 (73), EEC Relations with Developing Countries, 2nd meeting, 19 January 1973.
10 Ibid., 3rd meeting, 29 January 1973.
11 NA, FCO 30/1688. Meeting between the Prime Minister and President Nixon. EEC Association for Developing Commonwealth Countries – Background, 24 January 1973.
12 NA, FCO 30/1694. Meetings of Claude Cheysson with the Chancellor of the Duchy of Lancaster (John Davies) and the Minister for Overseas Development (Richard Wood), 24 May 1973.
13 Ibid.
14 NA, FCO 30/1690. R.S. Fairweather, Overseas Development Administration, to D.J.E Ratford, 15 February 1973.

15 NA, FCO 30/1690. S.J.G. Cambridge (Rome Embassy) to J.A. Robinson (European Integration Department), 20 February 1973.

16 NA, FCO 30/1694. Summary record of Ministers' discussion with M. Cheysson, 24 May 1973. Maurice Foley, Assistant Director of D.G.VIII, present at the meeting, said that it was up to the United Kingdom to make a proposal for getting around GATT.

17 NA, FCO 30/1693. Visit of M. Cheysson, 24 May 1973, Protocol 22, speaking note.

18 NA, FCO 30/1693. Ibid., 'Detailed argument on why we have taken this stand on reciprocity – for use if required'.

19 NA, FCO 30/1694. Telegram from Brussels. Heath–Pompidou meeting, 21–22 May 1973.

20 NA, FCO 30/1693. Meeting of the Council of Ministers of the European Community, 14 May 1973.

21 Ibid., J.A. Robinson (European Integration Department) to B.C. Cubbon (Cabinet Office), 14 May 1973.

22 NA, FCO 30/1690. R.G. Denman (DTI) to B.C. Cubbon (Cabinet Office), 14 March 1973.

23 NA, FCO 30/1693. M. Palliser (UKREP, Brussels) to FCO, 25 May.

24 It was Ivar Norgaard, Krag's Minister for External Economic Affairs.

25 NA, FCO 30/1695. Telegram, Palliser (UKREP) to FCO, 28 July 1973.

26 Ibid.

27 NA, PREM 15/360. Telegram, Paris Embassy to FCO, 23 March 1971.

28 NA, FCO 30/1688. Meeting between the Prime Minister and President Nixon. EEC Association for Developing Countries – background (n.d.)

29 NA, FCO 30/1891. Memorandum, D.M. Kerr (Financial Relations Dept.) to D.J.E. Ratford (European Integration Dept.), 17 April 1973.

30 T.M. Shaw, 'EEC–ACP interactions and images as redefinitions of Eur-Africa: exemplary, exclusive and/or exploitative', *Journal of Common Market Studies*, 18(2) (December 1979) pp. 135–58.

31 A. Sapir, 'Trade benefits under the EEC generalized system of preferences', *European Economic Review*, 3 (June 1981), pp. 339–55.

32 R.J. Langhammer and A. Sapir, *Economic Impact of Generalized Tariff Preferences* (Aldershot: Gower, 1987), p. 37.

33 For an attempt to bring the various sociological, anthropological and economic viewpoints about economic development under the Lomé regime into perspective, S. Mapp (ed.) *Ambitions et illusions de la co-opération Nord–Sud: Lomé IV* (Paris: Harmattan, 1990).

34 V. Dimier, *Le gouvernement des colonies, regards croisés franco-britanniques* (Brussels: Éditions de l'Université de Bruxelles, 2004), passim. Idem. *Le discourse idéologique de la méthode coloniale chez les Français et les Britanniques de l'entre-deux-guerres à la décolonisation (1920–1960)* (Brussels: Talence, 1998).

35 'Commission, Court and Parliament have indeed served repeatedly as "engines of integration"… exerting an independent causal impact on EU policy outcomes and pushing forward both the creation and the regulation of the Single European Market. In this sense the supranationalist vision of leaders such as Jean Monnet and Walter Hallstein, as well as the neo-functionalist integration theories of Ernst Haas and others, have been largely vindicated.' M.A. Pollack, *The Engines of European Integration: Delegation, Agency, and Agenda Setting in the EU* (New York: Oxford University Press, 2003), p. 390.

Index

.

Printed in the United States
by Baker & Taylor Publisher Services